THE INTELLIGENT INVESTORS

CORRECT INVESTMENT STRATEGY
HOW TO INVEST WISELY (VOL.3)

- KRISTINA HARRIS -

CONTENT

The text reproduced here is the Fourth Revised Edition, updated by Graham in 1971–1972 and initially published in 1973. Please be advised that the text of Graham's original footnotes (designated in his chapters with superscript numerals) can be found in the Endnotes section beginning on p. 579. The new footnotes that Jason Zweig has introduced appear at the bottom of Graham's pages (and, in the typeface used here, as occasional additions to Graham's endnotes).

INTRODUCTION:

What This Book Expects to Accomplish

*T*he purpose of this book is to supply, in a form suitable for laymen, guidance in the adoption and execution of an investment policy. Comparatively little will be said here about the technique of analyzing securities; attention will be paid chiefly to investment principles and investors' attitudes. We shall, however, provide a number of condensed comparisons of specific securities—chiefly in pairs appearing side by side in the New York Stock Exchange list—in order to bring home in concrete fashion the important elements involved in specific choices of common stocks.

But much of our space will be devoted to the historical patterns of financial markets, in some cases running back over many decades. To invest intelligently in securities one should be forearmed with an adequate knowledge of how the various types of bonds and stocks have actually behaved under varying conditions—some of which, at least, one is likely to meet again in one's own experience. No statement is more true and better applicable to Wall Street than the famous warning of Santayana: "Those who do not remember the past are condemned to repeat it."

Our text is directed to investors as distinguished from speculators, and our first task will be to clarify and emphasize this now all but forgotten distinction. We may say at the outset that this is not a "how to make a million" book. There are no sure and easy paths to riches on Wall Street or anywhere else. It may be well to point up what we have just said by a bit of financial history—especially since there is more than one moral to be drawn from it. In the climactic year 1929 John J. Raskob, a most important figure nationally as well as on Wall Street, extolled the blessings of capitalism in an article in the *Ladies' Home Journal*, entitled "Everybody Ought to Be

Rich."* His thesis was that savings of only \$15 per month invested in good common stocks—with dividends reinvested—would produce an estate of \$80,000 in twenty years against total contributions of only \$3,600. If the General Motors tycoon was right, this was indeed a simple road to riches. How nearly right was he? Our rough calculation—based on assumed investment in the 30 stocks making up the Dow Jones Industrial Average (DJIA)—indicates that if Raskob's prescription had been followed during 1929–1948, the investor's holdings at the beginning of 1949 would have been worth about \$8,500. This is a far cry from the great man's promise of \$80,000, and it shows how little reliance can be placed on such optimistic forecasts and assurances. But, as an aside, we should remark that the return actually realized by the 20-year operation would have been better than 8% compounded annually—and this despite the fact that the investor would have begun his purchases with the DJIA at 300 and ended with a valuation based on the 1948 closing level of 177. This record may be regarded as a persuasive argument for the principle of regular monthly purchases of strong common stocks through thick and thin—a program known as "dollar-cost averaging."

Since our book is not addressed to speculators, it is not meant for those who trade in the market. Most of these people are guided by charts or other largely mechanical means of determining the right moments to buy and sell. The one principle that applies to nearly all these so-called "technical approaches" is that one should buy *because* a stock or the market has gone up and one should sell *because* it has declined. This is the exact opposite of sound business sense everywhere else, and it is most unlikely that it can lead to

---

* Raskob (1879–1950) was a director of Du Pont, the giant chemical company, and chairman of the finance committee at General Motors. He also served as national chairman of the Democratic Party and was the driving force behind the construction of the Empire State Building. Calculations by finance professor Jeremy Siegel confirm that Raskob's plan would have grown to just under \$9,000 after 20 years, although inflation would have eaten away much of that gain. For the best recent look at Raskob's views on long-term stock investing, see the essay by financial adviser William Bernstein at www.efficientfrontier.com/ef/197/raskob.htm.

lasting success on Wall Street. In our own stock-market experience and observation, extending over 50 years, we have not known a single person who has consistently or lastingly made money by thus "following the market." We do not hesitate to declare that this approach is as fallacious as it is popular. We shall illustrate what we have just said—though, of course this should not be taken as proof—by a later brief discussion of the famous Dow theory for trading in the stock market.*

Since its first publication in 1949, revisions of *The Intelligent Investor* have appeared at intervals of approximately five years. In updating the current version we shall have to deal with quite a number of new developments since the 1965 edition was written. These include:

1. An unprecedented advance in the interest rate on high-grade bonds.
2. A fall of about 35% in the price level of leading common stocks, ending in May 1970. This was the highest percentage decline in some 30 years. (Countless issues of lower quality had a much larger shrinkage.)
3. A persistent inflation of wholesale and consumer's prices, which gained momentum even in the face of a decline of general business in 1970.
4. The rapid development of "conglomerate" companies, franchise operations, and other relative novelties in business and finance. (These include a number of tricky devices such as "letter stock,"[1] proliferation of stock-option warrants, misleading names, use of foreign banks, and others.)†

---

* Graham's "brief discussion" is in two parts, on p. 33 and pp. 191–192. For more detail on the Dow Theory, see http://viking.som.yale.edu/will/dow/dowpage.html.

† Mutual funds bought "letter stock" in private transactions, then immediately revalued these shares at a higher public price (see Graham's definition on p. 579). That enabled these "go-go" funds to report unsustainably high returns in the mid-1960s. The U.S. Securities and Exchange Commission cracked down on this abuse in 1969, and it is no longer a concern for fund investors. Stock-option warrants are explained in Chapter 16.

5. Bankruptcy of our largest railroad, excessive short- and long-
    term debt of many formerly strongly entrenched companies,
    and even a disturbing problem of solvency among Wall Street
    houses.*
6. The advent of the "performance" vogue in the management of
    investment funds, including some bank-operated trust funds,
    with disquieting results.

These phenomena will have our careful consideration, and some
will require changes in conclusions and emphasis from our previous edition. The underlying principles of sound investment should
not alter from decade to decade, but the application of these principles must be adapted to significant changes in the financial mecha-
nisms and climate.

The last statement was put to the test during the writing of the
present edition, the first draft of which was finished in January
1971. At that time the DJIA was in a strong recovery from its 1970
low of 632 and was advancing toward a 1971 high of 951, with
attendant general optimism. As the last draft was finished, in
November 1971, the market was in the throes of a new decline, car-
rying it down to 797 with a renewed general uneasiness about its
future. We have not allowed these fluctuations to affect our general
attitude toward sound investment policy, which remains substantially unchanged since the first edition of this book in 1949.

The extent of the market's shrinkage in 1969–70 should have
served to dispel an illusion that had been gaining ground during the past two decades. This was that leading common stocks
could be bought at any time and at any price, with the assurance not
only of ultimate profit but also that any intervening loss would soon
be recouped by a renewed advance of the market to new high lev-

---

* The Penn Central Transportation Co., then the biggest railroad in the
United States, sought bankruptcy protection on June 21, 1970–shocking
investors, who had never expected such a giant company to go under (see
p. 423). Among the companies with "excessive" debt Graham had in mind
were Ling-Temco-Vought and National General Corp. (see pp. 425 and
463). The "problem of solvency" on Wall Street emerged between 1968
and 1971, when several prestigious brokerages suddenly went bust.

els. That was too good to be true. At long last the stock market has "returned to normal," in the sense that both speculators and stock investors must again be prepared to experience significant and perhaps protracted falls as well as rises in the value of their holdings.

In the area of many secondary and third-line common stocks, especially recently floated enterprises, the havoc wrought by the last market break was catastrophic. This was nothing new in itself—it had happened to a similar degree in 1961–62—but there was now a novel element in the fact that some of the investment funds had large commitments in highly speculative and obviously overvalued issues of this type. Evidently it is not only the tyro who needs to be warned that while enthusiasm may be necessary for great accomplishments elsewhere, on Wall Street it almost invariably leads to disaster.

The major question we shall have to deal with grows out of the huge rise in the rate of interest on first-quality bonds. Since late 1967 the investor has been able to obtain more than twice as much income from such bonds as he could from dividends on representative common stocks. At the beginning of 1972 the return was 7.19% on highest-grade bonds versus only 2.76% on industrial stocks. (This compares with 4.40% and 2.92% respectively at the end of 1964.) It is hard to realize that when we first wrote this book in 1949 the figures were almost the exact opposite: the bonds returned only 2.66% and the stocks yielded 6.82%.[2] In previous editions we have consistently urged that at least 25% of the conservative investor's portfolio be held in common stocks, and we have favored in general a 50–50 division between the two media. We must now consider whether the current great advantage of bond yields over stock yields would justify an all-bond policy until a more sensible relationship returns, as we expect it will. Naturally the question of continued inflation will be of great importance in reaching our decision here. A chapter will be devoted to this discussion.*

---

* See Chapter 2. As of the beginning of 2003, U.S. Treasury bonds maturing in 10 years yielded 3.8%, while stocks (as measured by the Dow Jones Industrial Average) yielded 1.9%. (Note that this relationship is not all that different from the 1964 figures that Graham cites.) The income generated by top-quality bonds has been falling steadily since 1981.

In the past we have made a basic distinction between two kinds of investors to whom this book was addressed—the "defensive" and the "enterprising." The defensive (or passive) investor will place his chief emphasis on the avoidance of serious mistakes or losses. His second aim will be freedom from effort, annoyance, and the need for making frequent decisions. The determining trait of the enterprising (or active, or aggressive) investor is his willingness to devote time and care to the selection of securities that are both sound and more attractive than the average. Over many decades an enterprising investor of this sort could expect a worthwhile reward for his extra skill and effort, in the form of a better average return than that realized by the passive investor. We have some doubt whether a really substantial extra recompense is promised to the active investor under today's conditions. But next year or the years after may well be different. We shall accordingly continue to devote attention to the possibilities for enterprising investment, as they existed in former periods and may return.

It has long been the prevalent view that the art of successful investment lies first in the choice of those industries that are most likely to grow in the future and then in identifying the most promising companies in these industries. For example, smart investors—or their smart advisers—would long ago have recognized the great growth possibilities of the computer industry as a whole and of International Business Machines in particular. And similarly for a number of other growth industries and growth companies. But this is not as easy as it always looks in retrospect. To bring this point home at the outset let us add here a paragraph that we included first in the 1949 edition of this book.

> Such an investor may for example be a buyer of air-transport stocks because he believes their future is even more brilliant than the trend the market already reflects. For this class of investor the value of our book will lie more in its warnings against the pitfalls lurking in this favorite investment approach than in any positive technique that will help him along his path.*

---

* "Air-transport stocks," of course, generated as much excitement in the late 1940s and early 1950s as Internet stocks did a half century later. Among the hottest mutual funds of that era were Aeronautical Securities and the

The pitfalls have proved particularly dangerous in the industry we mentioned. It was, of course, easy to forecast that the volume of air traffic would grow spectacularly over the years. Because of this factor their shares became a favorite choice of the investment funds. But despite the expansion of revenues—at a pace even greater than in the computer industry—a combination of technological problems and overexpansion of capacity made for fluctuating and even disastrous profit figures. In the year 1970, despite a new high in traffic figures, the airlines sustained a loss of some $200 million for their shareholders. (They had shown losses also in 1945 and 1961.) The stocks of these companies once again showed a greater decline in 1969–70 than did the general market. The record shows that even the highly paid full-time experts of the mutual funds were completely wrong about the fairly short-term future of a major and nonesoteric industry.

On the other hand, while the investment funds had substantial investments and substantial gains in IBM, the combination of its apparently high price and the impossibility of being *certain* about its rate of growth prevented them from having more than, say, 3% of their funds in this wonderful performer. Hence the effect of this excellent choice on their overall results was by no means decisive. Furthermore, many—if not most—of their investments in computer-industry companies other than IBM appear to have been unprofitable. From these two broad examples we draw two morals for our readers:

1. Obvious prospects for physical growth in a business do not translate into obvious profits for investors.
2. The experts do not have dependable ways of selecting and concentrating on the most promising companies in the most promising industries.

Missiles-Rockets-Jets & Automation Fund. They, like the stocks they owned, turned out to be an investing disaster. It is commonly accepted today that the cumulative earnings of the airline industry over its entire history have been negative. The lesson Graham is driving at is not that you should avoid buying airline stocks, but that you should never succumb to the "certainty" that any industry will outperform all others in the future.

The author did not follow this approach in his financial career as fund manager, and he cannot offer either specific counsel or much encouragement to those who may wish to try it.

What then will we aim to accomplish in this book? Our main objective will be to guide the reader against the areas of possible substantial error and to develop policies with which he will be comfortable. We shall say quite a bit about the psychology of investors. For indeed, the investor's chief problem—and even his worst enemy—is likely to be himself. ("The fault, dear investor, is not in our stars—and not in our stocks—but in ourselves. . . .") This has proved the more true over recent decades as it has become more necessary for conservative investors to acquire common stocks and thus to expose themselves, willy-nilly, to the excitement and the temptations of the stock market. By arguments, examples, and exhortation, we hope to aid our readers to establish the proper mental and emotional attitudes toward their investment decisions. We have seen much more money made and *kept* by "ordinary people" who were temperamentally well suited for the investment process than by those who lacked this quality, even though they had an extensive knowledge of finance, accounting, and stock-market lore.

Additionally, we hope to implant in the reader a tendency to measure or quantify. For 99 issues out of 100 we could say that at some price they are cheap enough to buy and at some other price they would be so dear that they should be sold. The habit of relating what is paid to what is being offered is an invaluable trait in investment. In an article in a women's magazine many years ago we advised the readers to buy their stocks as they bought their groceries, not as they bought their perfume. The really dreadful losses of the past few years (and on many similar occasions before) were realized in those common-stock issues where the buyer forgot to ask "How much?"

In June 1970 the question "How much?" could be answered by the magic figure 9.40%—the yield obtainable on new offerings of high-grade public-utility bonds. This has now dropped to about 7.3%, but even that return tempts us to ask, "Why give any other answer?" But there are other possible answers, and these must be carefully considered. Besides which, we repeat that both we and our readers must be prepared in advance for the possibly quite different conditions of, say, 1973–1977.

We shall therefore present in some detail a positive program for common-stock investment, part of which is within the purview of both classes of investors and part is intended mainly for the enterprising group. Strangely enough, we shall suggest as one of our chief requirements here that our readers limit themselves to issues selling not far above their tangible-asset value.* The reason for this seemingly outmoded counsel is both practical and psychological. Experience has taught us that, while there are many good growth companies worth several times net assets, the buyer of such shares will be too dependent on the vagaries and fluctuations of the stock market. By contrast, the investor in shares, say, of public-utility companies at about their net-asset value can always consider himself the owner of an interest in sound and expanding businesses, acquired at a rational price—regardless of what the stock market might say to the contrary. The ultimate result of such a conservative policy is likely to work out better than exciting adventures into the glamorous and dangerous fields of anticipated growth.

The art of investment has one characteristic that is not generally appreciated. A creditable, if unspectacular, result can be achieved by the lay investor with a minimum of effort and capability; but to improve this easily attainable standard requires much application and more than a trace of wisdom. If you merely try to bring *just a little* extra knowledge and cleverness to bear upon your investment program, instead of realizing a little better than normal results, you may well find that you have done worse.

Since anyone—by just buying and holding a representative list—can equal the performance of the market averages, it would seem a comparatively simple matter to "beat the averages"; but as a matter of fact the proportion of smart people who try this and fail is surprisingly large. Even the majority of the investment funds, with all their experienced personnel, have not performed so well

---

* Tangible assets include a company's physical property (like real estate, factories, equipment, and inventories) as well as its financial balances (such as cash, short-term investments, and accounts receivable). Among the elements not included in tangible assets are brands, copyrights, patents, franchises, goodwill, and trademarks. To see how to calculate tangible-asset value, see footnote † on p. 198.

over the years as has the general market. Allied to the foregoing is the record of the published stock-market predictions of the brokerage houses, for there is strong evidence that their calculated forecasts have been somewhat less reliable than the simple tossing of a coin.

In writing this book we have tried to keep this basic pitfall of investment in mind. The virtues of a simple portfolio policy have been emphasized—the purchase of high-grade bonds plus a diversified list of leading common stocks—which any investor can carry out with a little expert assistance. The adventure beyond this safe and sound territory has been presented as fraught with challenging difficulties, especially in the area of temperament. Before attempting such a venture the investor should feel sure of himself and of his advisers—particularly as to whether they have a clear concept of the differences between investment and speculation and between market price and underlying value.

A strong-minded approach to investment, firmly based on the margin-of-safety principle, can yield handsome rewards. But a decision to try for these emoluments rather than for the assured fruits of defensive investment should not be made without much self-examination.

A final retrospective thought. When the young author entered Wall Street in June 1914 no one had any inkling of what the next half-century had in store. (The stock market did not even suspect that a World War was to break out in two months, and close down the New York Stock Exchange.) Now, in 1972, we find ourselves the richest and most powerful country on earth, but beset by all sorts of major problems and more apprehensive than confident of the future. Yet if we confine our attention to American investment experience, there is some comfort to be gleaned from the last 57 years. Through all their vicissitudes and casualties, as earth-shaking as they were unforeseen, it remained true that sound investment principles produced generally sound results. We must act on the assumption that they will continue to do so.

Note to the Reader: This book does not address itself to the *overall* financial policy of savers and investors; it deals only with that portion of their funds which they are prepared to place in marketable (or redeemable) securities, that is, in bonds and stocks.

Consequently we do not discuss such important media as savings and time desposits, savings-and-loan-association accounts, life insurance, annuities, and real-estate mortgages or equity ownership. The reader should bear in mind that when he finds the word "now," or the equivalent, in the text, it refers to late 1971 or early 1972.

COMMENTARY ON CHAPTER 8

The happiness of those who want to be popular depends on others; the happiness of those who seek pleasure fluctuates with moods outside their control; but the happiness of the wise grows out of their own free acts.

—*Marcus Aurelius*

DR. JEKYLL AND MR. MARKET

Most of the time, the market is mostly accurate in pricing most stocks. Millions of buyers and sellers haggling over price do a remarkably good job of valuing companies—on average. But sometimes, the price is not right; occasionally, it is very wrong indeed. And at such times, you need to understand Graham's image of Mr. Market, probably the most brilliant metaphor ever created for explaining how stocks can become mispriced.[1] The manic-depressive Mr. Market does not always price stocks the way an appraiser or a private buyer would value a business. Instead, when stocks are going up, he happily pays more than their objective value; and, when they are going down, he is desperate to dump them for less than their true worth.

Is Mr. Market still around? Is he still bipolar? You bet he is.

On March 17, 2000, the stock of Inktomi Corp. hit a new high of $231.625. Since they first came on the market in June 1998, shares in the Internet-searching software company had gained roughly 1,900%. Just in the few weeks since December 1999, the stock had nearly tripled.

What was going on at Inktomi the business that could make Inktomi the stock so valuable? The answer seems obvious: phenomenally fast

---

[1] See Graham's text, pp. 204–205.

growth. In the three months ending in December 1999, Inktomi sold $36 million in products and services, more than it had in the entire year ending in December 1998. If Inktomi could sustain its growth rate of the previous 12 months for just five more years, its revenues would explode from $36 million a quarter to $5 billion a month. With such growth in sight, the faster the stock went up, the farther up it seemed certain to go.

But in his wild love affair with Inktomi's stock, Mr. Market was overlooking something about its business. The company was losing money—lots of it. It had lost $6 million in the most recent quarter, $24 million in the 12 months before that, and $24 million in the year before that. In its entire corporate lifetime, Inktomi had never made a dime in profits. Yet, on March 17, 2000, Mr. Market valued this tiny business at a total of $25 billion. (Yes, that's *billion,* with a *B*.)

And then Mr. Market went into a sudden, nightmarish depression. On September 30, 2002, just two and a half years after hitting $231.625 per share, Inktomi's stock closed at 25 cents—collapsing from a total market value of $25 billion to less than $40 million. Had Inktomi's business dried up? Not at all; over the previous 12 months, the company had generated $113 million in revenues. So what had changed? Only Mr. Market's mood: In early 2000, investors were so wild about the Internet that they priced Inktomi's shares at 250 times the company's revenues. Now, however, they would pay only 0.35 times its revenues. Mr. Market had morphed from Dr. Jekyll to Mr. Hyde and was ferociously trashing every stock that had made a fool out of him.

But Mr. Market was no more justified in his midnight rage than he had been in his manic euphoria. On December 23, 2002, Yahoo! Inc. announced that it would buy Inktomi for $1.65 per share. That was nearly seven times Inktomi's stock price on September 30. History will probably show that Yahoo! got a bargain. When Mr. Market makes stocks so cheap, it's no wonder that entire companies get bought right out from under him.[2]

---

[2] As Graham noted in a classic series of articles in 1932, the Great Depression caused the shares of dozens of companies to drop below the value of their cash and other liquid assets, making them "worth more dead than alive."

THINK FOR YOURSELF

Would you willingly allow a certifiable lunatic to come by at least five times a week to tell you that you should feel exactly the way he feels? Would you ever agree to be euphoric just because he is—or miserable just because he thinks you should be? Of course not. You'd insist on your right to take control of your own emotional life, based on your experiences and your beliefs. But, when it comes to their financial lives, millions of people let Mr. Market tell them how to feel and what to do—despite the obvious fact that, from time to time, he can get nuttier than a fruitcake.

In 1999, when Mr. Market was squealing with delight, American employees directed an average of 8.6% of their paychecks into their 401(k) retirement plans. By 2002, after Mr. Market had spent three years stuffing stocks into black garbage bags, the average contribution rate had dropped by nearly one-quarter, to just 7%.[3] The cheaper stocks got, the less eager people became to buy them—because they were imitating Mr. Market, instead of thinking for themselves.

The intelligent investor shouldn't ignore Mr. Market entirely. Instead, you should do business with him—but only to the extent that it serves your interests. Mr. Market's job is to provide you with prices; your job is to decide whether it is to your advantage to act on them. *You do not have to trade with him just because he constantly begs you to.*

By refusing to let Mr. Market be your master, you transform him into your servant. After all, even when he seems to be destroying values, he is creating them elsewhere. In 1999, the Wilshire 5000 index—the broadest measure of U.S. stock performance—gained 23.8%, powered by technology and telecommunications stocks. But 3,743 of the 7,234 stocks in the Wilshire index went down in value even as the average was rising. While those high-tech and telecom stocks were hotter than the hood of a race car on an August afternoon, thousands of "Old Economy" shares were frozen in the mud—getting cheaper and cheaper.

The stock of CMGI, an "incubator" or holding company for Internet

---

[3] News release, The Spectrem Group, "Plan Sponsors Are Losing the Battle to Prevent Declining Participation and Deferrals into Defined Contribution Plans," October 25, 2002.

FIGURE 8-1   From Stinkers to Stars

Company	Business	Total Return				Final value of $1,000 invested 1/1/1999
		1999	2000	2001	2002	
Angelica	industrial uniforms	–43.7	1.8	19.3	94.1	1,328
Ball Corp.	metal & plastic packaging	–12.7	19.2	55.3	46.0	2,359
Checkers Drive-In Restaurants	fast food	–45.5	63.9	66.2	2.1	1,517
Family Dollar Stores	discount retailer	–25.1	33.0	41.1	5.0	1,476
International Game Technology	gambling equipment	–16.3	136.1	42.3	11.2	3,127
J B Hunt Transportation	trucking	–39.1	21.9	38.0	26.3	1,294
Jos. A. Bank Clothiers	apparel	–62.5	50.0	57.1	201.6	2,665
Lockheed Martin	defense & aerospace	–46.9	58.0	39.0	24.7	1,453
Pier 1 Imports	home furnishings	–33.2	63.9	70.5	10.3	2,059
UST Inc.	snuff tobacco	–23.5	21.6	32.2	1.0	1,241
Wilshire Internet Index		139.1	–55.5	–46.2	–45.0	315
Wilshire 5000 index (total stock market)		23.8	–10.9	–11.0	–20.8	778

Sources: Aronson + Johnson + Ortiz, L.P.; www.wilshire.com

start-up firms, went up an astonishing 939.9% in 1999. Meanwhile, Berkshire Hathaway—the holding company through which Graham's greatest disciple, Warren Buffett, owns such Old Economy stalwarts as Coca-Cola, Gillette, and the Washington Post Co.—dropped by 24.9%.[4]

But then, as it so often does, the market had a sudden mood swing. Figure 8-1 offers a sampling of how the stinkers of 1999 became the stars of 2000 through 2002.

As for those two holding companies, CMGI went on to lose 96% in 2000, another 70.9% in 2001, and still 39.8% more in 2002—a cumulative loss of 99.3%. Berkshire Hathaway went up 26.6% in 2000 and 6.5% in 2001, then had a slight 3.8% loss in 2002—a cumulative gain of 30%.

CAN YOU BEAT THE PROS AT THEIR OWN GAME?

One of Graham's most powerful insights is this: "The investor who permits himself to be stampeded or unduly worried by unjustified market declines in his holdings is perversely transforming his basic advantage into a basic disadvantage."

What does Graham mean by those words "basic advantage"? He means that the intelligent individual investor has the full freedom to choose whether or not to follow Mr. Market. You have the luxury of being able to think for yourself.[5]

---

[4] A few months later, on March 10, 2000—the very day that NASDAQ hit its all-time high—online trading pundit James J. Cramer wrote that he had "repeatedly" been tempted in recent days to sell Berkshire Hathaway short, a bet that Buffett's stock had farther to fall. With a vulgar thrust of his rhetorical pelvis, Cramer even declared that Berkshire's shares were "ripe for the banging." That same day, market strategist Ralph Acampora of Prudential Securities asked, "Norfolk Southern or Cisco Systems: Where do you want to be in the future?" Cisco, a key to tomorrow's Internet superhighway, seemed to have it all over Norfolk Southern, part of yesterday's railroad system. (Over the next year, Norfolk Southern gained 35%, while Cisco lost 70%.)

[5] When asked what keeps most individual investors from succeeding, Graham had a concise answer: "The primary cause of failure is that they pay too much attention to what the stock market is doing currently." See "Benjamin Graham: Thoughts on Security Analysis" [transcript of lecture at Northeast Missouri State University Business School, March, 1972], *Financial History* magazine, no. 42, March, 1991, p. 8.

The typical money manager, however, has no choice but to mimic Mr. Market's every move—buying high, selling low, marching almost mindlessly in his erratic footsteps. Here are some of the handicaps mutual-fund managers and other professional investors are saddled with:

- With billions of dollars under management, they must gravitate toward the biggest stocks—the only ones they can buy in the multimillion-dollar quantities they need to fill their portfolios. Thus many funds end up owning the same few overpriced giants.

- Investors tend to pour more money into funds as the market rises. The managers use that new cash to buy more of the stocks they already own, driving prices to even more dangerous heights.

- If fund investors ask for their money back when the market drops, the managers may need to sell stocks to cash them out. Just as the funds are forced to buy stocks at inflated prices in a rising market, they become forced sellers as stocks get cheap again.

- Many portfolio managers get bonuses for beating the market, so they obsessively measure their returns against benchmarks like the S & P 500 index. If a company gets added to an index, hundreds of funds compulsively buy it. (If they don't, and that stock then does well, the managers look foolish; on the other hand, if they buy it and it does poorly, no one will blame them.)

- Increasingly, fund managers are expected to specialize. Just as in medicine the general practitioner has given way to the pediatric allergist and the geriatric otolaryngologist, fund managers must buy only "small growth" stocks, or only "mid-sized value" stocks, or nothing but "large blend" stocks.[6] If a company gets too big, or too small, or too cheap, or an itty bit too expensive, the fund has to sell it—even if the manager loves the stock.

So there's no reason you can't do as well as the pros. What you cannot do (despite all the pundits who say you can) is to "beat the pros at their own game." *The pros can't even win their own game!* Why should you want to play it at all? If you follow their rules, you will lose—since you will end up as much a slave to Mr. Market as the professionals are.

---

[6] Never mind what these terms mean, or are supposed to mean. While in public these classifications are treated with the utmost respect, in private most people in the investment business regard them with the contempt normally reserved for jokes that aren't funny.

Instead, recognize that investing intelligently is about controlling the controllable. You can't control whether the stocks or funds you buy will outperform the market today, next week, this month, or this year; in the short run, your returns will always be hostage to Mr. Market and his whims. But you *can* control:

- **your brokerage costs,** by trading rarely, patiently, and cheaply
- **your ownership costs,** by refusing to buy mutual funds with excessive annual expenses
- **your expectations,** by using realism, not fantasy, to forecast your returns[7]
- **your risk,** by deciding how much of your total assets to put at hazard in the stock market, by diversifying, and by rebalancing
- **your tax bills,** by holding stocks for at least one year and, whenever possible, for at least five years, to lower your capital-gains liability
- and, most of all, **your own behavior.**

If you listen to financial TV, or read most market columnists, you'd think that investing is some kind of sport, or a war, or a struggle for survival in a hostile wilderness. *But investing isn't about beating others at their game. It's about controlling yourself at your own game.* The challenge for the intelligent investor is not to find the stocks that will go up the most and down the least, but rather to prevent yourself from being your own worst enemy—from buying high just because Mr. Market says "Buy!" and from selling low just because Mr. Market says "Sell!"

If you investment horizon is long—at least 25 or 30 years—there is only one sensible approach: Buy every month, automatically, and whenever else you can spare some money. The single best choice for this lifelong holding is a total stock-market index fund. Sell only when you need the cash (for a psychological boost, clip out and sign your "Investment Owner's Contract"—which you can find on p. 225).

To be an intelligent investor, you must also refuse to judge your financial success by how a bunch of total strangers are doing. You're not one penny poorer if someone in Dubuque or Dallas or Denver

---

[7] See the brilliant column by Walter Updegrave, "Keep It Real," *Money,* February, 2002, pp. 53–56.

beats the S & P 500 and you don't. No one's gravestone reads "HE BEAT THE MARKET."

I once interviewed a group of retirees in Boca Raton, one of Florida's wealthiest retirement communities. I asked these people—mostly in their seventies—if they had beaten the market over their investing lifetimes. Some said yes, some said no; most weren't sure. Then one man said, "Who cares? All I know is, my investments earned enough for me to end up in Boca."

Could there be a more perfect answer? After all, the whole point of investing is not to earn more money than average, but to earn enough money to meet your own needs. The best way to measure your investing success is not by whether you're beating the market but by whether you've put in place a financial plan and a behavioral discipline that are likely to get you where you want to go. In the end, what matters isn't crossing the finish line before anybody else but just making sure that you do cross it.[8]

YOUR MONEY AND YOUR BRAIN

Why, then, do investors find Mr. Market so seductive? It turns out that our brains are hardwired to get us into investing trouble; humans are pattern-seeking animals. Psychologists have shown that if you present people with a random sequence—and tell them that it's unpredictable—they will nevertheless insist on trying to guess what's coming next. Likewise, we "know" that the next roll of the dice will be a seven, that a baseball player is due for a base hit, that the next winning number in the Powerball lottery will definitely be 4-27-9-16-42-10—and that this hot little stock is the next Microsoft.

Groundbreaking new research in neuroscience shows that our brains are designed to perceive trends even where they might not exist. After an event occurs just two or three times in a row, regions of the human brain called the anterior cingulate and nucleus accumbens automatically anticipate that it will happen again. If it does repeat, a natural chemical called dopamine is released, flooding your brain with a soft euphoria. Thus, if a stock goes up a few times in a row, you reflexively expect it to keep going—and your brain chemistry changes

---

[8] See Jason Zweig, "Did You Beat the Market?" *Money*, January, 2000, pp. 55–58.

as the stock rises, giving you a "natural high." You effectively become addicted to your own predictions.

But when stocks drop, that financial loss fires up your amygdala–the part of the brain that processes fear and anxiety and generates the famous "fight or flight" response that is common to all cornered animals. Just as you can't keep your heart rate from rising if a fire alarm goes off, just as you can't avoid flinching if a rattlesnake slithers onto your hiking path, you can't help feeling fearful when stock prices are plunging.[9]

In fact, the brilliant psychologists Daniel Kahneman and Amos Tversky have shown that the pain of financial loss is more than twice as intense as the pleasure of an equivalent gain. Making $1,000 on a stock feels great–but a $1,000 loss wields an emotional wallop more than twice as powerful. Losing money is so painful that many people, terrified at the prospect of any further loss, sell out near the bottom or refuse to buy more.

That helps explain why we fixate on the raw magnitude of a market decline and forget to put the loss in proportion. So, if a TV reporter hollers, "The market is *plunging*–the Dow is down *100 points!*" most people instinctively shudder. But, at the Dow's recent level of 8,000, that's a drop of just 1.2%. Now think how ridiculous it would sound if, on a day when it's 81 degrees outside, the TV weatherman shrieked, "The temperature is *plunging*–it's dropped from *81 degrees* to *80 degrees!*" That, too, is a 1.2% drop. When you forget to view changing market prices in percentage terms, it's all too easy to panic over minor vibrations. (If you have decades of investing ahead of you, there's a better way to visualize the financial news broadcasts; see the sidebar on p. 222.)

In the late 1990s, many people came to feel that they were in the dark unless they checked the prices of their stocks several times a day. But, as Graham puts it, the typical investor "would be better off if his stocks had no market quotation at all, for he would then be spared the mental anguish caused him by *other persons'* mistakes of judg-

---

[9] The neuroscience of investing is explored in Jason Zweig, "Are You Wired for Wealth?" *Money,* October, 2002, pp. 74–83, also available at http:// money.cnn.com/2002/09/25/pf/investing/agenda_brain _short/index.htm. See also Jason Zweig, "The Trouble with Humans," *Money,* November, 2000, pp. 67–70.

NEWS YOU COULD USE

Stocks are crashing, so you turn on the television to catch the latest market news. But instead of CNBC or CNN, imagine that you can tune in to the Benjamin Graham Financial Network. On BGFN, the audio doesn't capture that famous sour clang of the market's closing bell; the video doesn't home in on brokers scurrying across the floor of the stock exchange like angry rodents. Nor does BGFN run any footage of investors gasping on frozen sidewalks as red arrows whiz overhead on electronic stock tickers.

Instead, the image that fills your TV screen is the facade of the New York Stock Exchange, festooned with a huge banner reading: "SALE! 50% OFF!" As intro music, Bachman-Turner Overdrive can be heard blaring a few bars of their old barn-burner, "You Ain't Seen Nothin' Yet." Then the anchorman announces brightly, "Stocks became more attractive *yet again* today, as the Dow dropped *another* 2.5% on heavy volume—the *fourth day in a row* that stocks have gotten *cheaper.* Tech investors fared *even better,* as leading companies like Microsoft *lost nearly 5% on the day,* making them *even more affordable.* That comes on *top* of the *good* news of the past year, in which stocks have *already* lost *50%,* putting them at *bargain* levels not seen in *years.* And *some* prominent analysts are *optimistic* that prices may drop *still further* in the weeks and months to come."

The newscast cuts over to market strategist Ignatz Anderson of the Wall Street firm of Ketchum & Skinner, who says, "My forecast is for stocks to lose *another 15%* by June. I'm cautiously *optimistic* that if *everything goes well,* stocks could lose *25%,* maybe *more.*"

"Let's hope Ignatz Anderson is *right,*" the anchor says cheerily. "*Falling* stock prices would be *fabulous* news for *any* investor with a very long *horizon.* And now over to *Wally Wood* for our *exclusive* AccuWeather forecast."

ment." If, after checking the value of your stock portfolio at 1:24 P.M., you feel compelled to check it all over again at 1:37 P.M., ask yourself these questions:

- Did I call a real-estate agent to check the market price of my house at 1:24 P.M.? Did I call back at 1:37 P.M.?
- If I had, would the price have changed? If it did, would I have rushed to sell my house?
- By not checking, or even knowing, the market price of my house from minute to minute, do I prevent its value from rising over time?[10]

The only possible answer to these questions is *of course not!* And you should view your portfolio the same way. Over a 10- or 20- or 30-year investment horizon, Mr. Market's daily dipsy-doodles simply do not matter. In any case, for anyone who will be investing for years to come, falling stock prices are good news, not bad, since they enable you to buy more for less money. The longer and further stocks fall, and the more steadily you keep buying as they drop, the more money you will make in the end—*if* you remain steadfast until the end. Instead of fearing a bear market, you should embrace it. The intelligent investor should be perfectly comfortable owning a stock or mutual fund even if the stock market stopped supplying daily prices for the next 10 years.[11]

Paradoxically, "you will be much more in control," explains neuroscientist Antonio Damasio, "if you realize how much you are not in control." By acknowledging your biological tendency to buy high and sell low, you can admit the need to dollar-cost average, rebalance, and sign an investment contract. By putting much of your portfolio on permanent autopilot, you can fight the prediction addiction, focus on your long-term financial goals, and tune out Mr. Market's mood swings.

---

[10] It's also worth asking whether you could enjoy living in your house if its market price was reported to the last penny every day in the newspapers and on TV.

[11] In a series of remarkable experiments in the late 1980s, a psychologist at Columbia and Harvard, Paul Andreassen, showed that investors who received frequent news updates on their stocks earned half the returns of investors who got no news at all. See Jason Zweig, "Here's How to Use the News and Tune Out the Noise," *Money,* July, 1998, pp. 63–64.

WHEN MR. MARKET GIVES YOU LEMONS, MAKE LEMONADE

Although Graham teaches that you should buy when Mr. Market is yelling "sell," there's one exception the intelligent investor needs to understand. Selling into a bear market can make sense if it creates a tax windfall. The U.S. Internal Revenue Code allows you to use your realized losses (any declines in value that you lock in by selling your shares) to offset up to $3,000 in ordinary income.[12] Let's say you bought 200 shares of Coca-Cola stock in January 2000 for $60 a share—a total investment of $12,000. By year-end 2002, the stock was down to $44 a share, or $8,800 for your lot—a loss of $3,200.

You could have done what most people do—either whine about your loss, or sweep it under the rug and pretend it never happened. Or you could have taken control. Before 2002 ended, you could have sold all your Coke shares, locking in the $3,200 loss. Then, after waiting 31 days to comply with IRS rules, you would buy 200 shares of Coke all over again. The result: You would be able to reduce your taxable income by $3,000 in 2002, and you could use the remaining $200 loss to offset your income in 2003. And better yet, you would still own a company whose future you believe in—but now you would own it for almost one-third less than you paid the first time.[13]

With Uncle Sam subsidizing your losses, it can make sense to sell and lock in a loss. If Uncle Sam wants to make Mr. Market look logical by comparison, who are we to complain?

---

[12] Federal tax law is subject to constant change. The example of Coca-Cola stock given here is valid under the provisions of the U.S. tax code as it stood in early 2003.

[13] This example assumes that the investor had no realized capital gains in 2002 and did not reinvest any Coke dividends. Tax swaps are not to be undertaken lightly, since they can be mishandled easily. Before doing a tax swap, read IRS Publication 550 (www.irs.gov/pub/irspdf/p550.pdf). A good guide to managing your investment taxes is Robert N. Gordon with Jan M. Rosen, *Wall Street Secrets for Tax-Efficient Investing* (Bloomberg Press, Princeton, New Jersey, 2001). Finally, before you pull the trigger, consult a professional tax adviser.

INVESTMENT OWNER'S CONTRACT

I, ________________ ____________________, hereby state that I am an investor who is seeking to accumulate wealth for many years into the future.

I know that there will be many times when I will be tempted to invest in stocks or bonds because they have gone (or "are going") up in price, and other times when I will be tempted to sell my investments because they have gone (or "are going") down.

I hereby declare my refusal to let a herd of strangers make my financial decisions for me. I further make a solemn commitment never to invest because the stock market has gone up, and never to sell because it has gone down. Instead, I will invest $______.00 per month, every month, through an automatic investment plan or "dollar-cost averaging program," into the following mutual fund(s) or diversified portfolio(s):

____,

____,

____.

I will also invest additional amounts whenever I can afford to spare the cash (and can afford to lose it in the short run).

I hereby declare that I will hold each of these investments continually through at least the following date (which must be a minimum of 10 years after the date of this contact): ____________________ ______, 20__. The only exceptions allowed under the terms of this contract are a sudden, pressing need for cash, like a health-care emergency or the loss of my job, or a planned expenditure like a housing down payment or a tuition bill.

I am, by signing below, stating my intention not only to abide by the terms of this contract, but to re-read this document whenever I am tempted to sell any of my investments.

This contract is valid only when signed by at least one witness, and must be kept in a safe place that is easily accessible for future reference.

Signed: Date:

____________________ ____________________   ____________________ ______, 20__

Witnesses:

____________________ ____________________

____________________ ____________________

CHAPTER 9

Investing in Investment Funds

One course open to the defensive investor is to put his money into investment-company shares. Those that are redeemable on demand by the holder, at net asset value, are commonly known as "mutual funds" (or "open-end funds"). Most of these are actively selling additional shares through a corps of salesmen. Those with nonredeemable shares are called "closed-end" companies or funds; the number of their shares remains relatively constant. All of the funds of any importance are registered with the Securities & Exchange Commission (SEC), and are subject to its regulations and controls.*

The industry is a very large one. At the end of 1970 there were 383 funds registered with the SEC, having assets totaling $54.6 billions. Of these 356 companies, with $50.6 billions, were mutual funds, and 27 companies with $4.0 billions, were closed-end.†

There are different ways of classifying the funds. One is by the broad division of their portfolio; they are "balanced funds" if they have a significant (generally about one-third) component of bonds, or "stock-funds" if their holdings are nearly all common stocks. (There are some other varieties here, such as "bond funds," "hedge

---

* It is a violation of Federal law for an open-end mutual fund, a closed-end fund, or an exchange-traded fund to sell shares to the public unless it has "registered" (or made mandatory financial filings) with the SEC.

† The fund industry has gone from "very large" to immense. At year-end 2002, there were 8,279 mutual funds holding $6.56 trillion; 514 closed-end funds with $149.6 billion in assets; and 116 exchange-trade funds or ETFs with $109.7 billion. These figures exclude such fund-like investments as variable annuities and unit investment trusts.

funds," "letter-stock funds," etc.)* Another is by their objectives, as their primary aim is for income, price stability, or capital appreciation ("growth"). Another distinction is by their method of sale. "Load funds" add a selling charge (generally about 9% of asset value on minimum purchases) to the value before charge.[1] Others, known as "no-load" funds, make no such charge; the managements are content with the usual investment-counsel fees for handling the capital. Since they cannot pay salesmen's commissions, the size of the no-load funds tends to be on the low side.† The buying and selling prices of the *closed-end* funds are not fixed by the companies, but fluctuate in the open market as does the ordinary corporate stock.

Most of the companies operate under special provisions of the income-tax law, designed to relieve the shareholders from double taxation on their earnings. In effect, the funds must pay out virtually all their ordinary income—i.e., dividends and interest received, less expenses. In addition they can pay out their realized long-term profits on sales of investments—in the form of "capital-gains dividends"—which are treated by the shareholder as if they were his own security profits. (There is another option here, which we omit to avoid clutter.)‡ Nearly all the funds have but one class

---

* Lists of the major types of mutual funds can be found at www.ici.org/pdf/g2understanding.pdf and http://news.morningstar.com/fundReturns/CategoryReturns.html. Letter-stock funds no longer exist, while hedge funds are generally banned by SEC rules from selling shares to any investor whose annual income is below $200,000 or whose net worth is below $1 million.

† Today, the maximum sales load on a stock fund tends to be around 5.75%. If you invest $10,000 in a fund with a flat 5.75% sales load, $575 will go to the person (and brokerage firm) that sold it to you, leaving you with an initial net investment of $9,425. The $575 sales charge is actually 6.1% of that amount, which is why Graham calls the standard way of calculating the charge a "sales gimmick." Since the 1980s, no-load funds have become popular, and they no longer tend to be smaller than load funds.

‡ Nearly every mutual fund today is taxed as a "regulated investment company," or RIC, which is exempt from corporate income tax so long as it pays out essentially all of its income to its shareholders. In the "option" that

of security outstanding. A new wrinkle, introduced in 1967, divides the capitalization into a preferred issue, which will receive all the ordinary income, and a capital issue, or common stock, which will receive all the profits on security sales. (These are called "dual-purpose funds.")*

Many of the companies that state their primary aim is for capital gains concentrate on the purchase of the so-called "growth stocks," and they often have the word "growth" in their name. Some specialize in a designated area such as chemicals, aviation, overseas investments; this is usually indicated in their titles.

The investor who wants to make an intelligent commitment in fund shares has thus a large and somewhat bewildering variety of choices before him—not too different from those offered in direct investment. In this chapter we shall deal with some major questions, viz:

1. Is there any way by which the investor can assure himself of better than average results by choosing the right funds? (Subquestion: What about the "performance funds"?)†

2. If not, how can he avoid choosing funds that will give him worse than average results?

3. Can he make intelligent choices between different types of funds—e.g., balanced versus all-stock, open-end versus closed-end, load versus no-load?

Graham omits "to avoid clutter," a fund can ask the SEC for special permission to distribute one of its holdings directly to the fund's shareholders—as his Graham-Newman Corp. did in 1948, parceling out shares in GEICO to Graham-Newman's own investors. This sort of distribution is extraordinarily rare.

* Dual-purpose funds, popular in the late 1980s, have essentially disappeared from the marketplace—a shame, since they offered investors a more flexible way to take advantage of the skills of great stock pickers like John Neff. Perhaps the recent bear market will lead to a renaissance of this attractive investment vehicle.

† "Performance funds" were all the rage in the late 1960s. They were equivalent to the aggressive growth funds of the late 1990s, and served their investors no better.

Investment-Fund Performance as a Whole

Before trying to answer these questions we should say something about the performance of the fund industry as a whole. Has it done a good job for its shareholders? In the most general way, how have fund investors fared as against those who made their investments directly? We are quite certain that the funds in the aggregate have served a useful purpose. They have promoted good habits of savings and investment; they have protected countless individuals against costly mistakes in the stock market; they have brought their participants income and profits commensurate with the overall returns from common stocks. On a comparative basis we would hazard the guess that the average individual who put his money exclusively in investment-fund shares in the past ten years has fared better than the average person who made his common-stock purchases directly.

The last point is probably true even though the actual performance of the funds seems to have been no better than that of common stocks as a whole, and even though the cost of investing in mutual funds may have been greater than that of direct purchases. The real choice of the average individual has not been between constructing and acquiring a well-balanced common-stock portfolio or doing the same thing, a bit more expensively, by buying into the funds. More likely his choice has been between succumbing to the wiles of the doorbell-ringing mutual-fund salesman on the one hand, as against succumbing to the even wilier and much more dangerous peddlers of second- and third-rate new offerings. We cannot help thinking, too, that the average individual who opens a brokerage account with the idea of making conservative common-stock investments is likely to find himself beset by untoward influences in the direction of speculation and speculative losses; these temptations should be much less for the mutual-fund buyer.

But how have the investment funds performed as against the general market? This is a somewhat controversial subject, but we shall try to deal with it in simple but adequate fashion. Table 9-1 gives some calculated results for 1961–1970 of our ten largest stock funds at the end of 1970, but choosing only the largest one from each management group. It summarizes the overall return of each of these funds for 1961–1965, 1966–1970, and for the single years

TABLE 9-1 Management Results of Ten Large Mutual Funds[a]

	(Indicated) 5 years, 1961–1965 (all +)	5 years, 1966–1970	10 years, 1961–1970 (all +)	1969	1970	Net Assets, December 1970 (millions)
Affiliated Fund	71%	+19.7%	105.3%	−14.3%	+2.2%	$1,600
Dreyfus	97	+18.7	135.4	−11.9	−6.4	2,232
Fidelity Fund	79	+31.8	137.1	−7.4	+2.2	819
Fundamental Inv.	79	+ 1.0	81.3	−12.7	−5.8	1,054
Invest. Co. of Am.	82	+37.9	152.2	−10.6	+2.3	1,168
Investors Stock Fund	54	+ 5.6	63.5	−80.0	−7.2	2,227
Mass. Inv. Trust	18	+16.2	44.2	− 4.0	+0.6	1,956
National Investors	61	+31.7	112.2	+ 4.0	−9.1	747
Putnam Growth	62	+22.3	104.0	−13.3	−3.8	684
United Accum.	74	− 2.0	72.7	−10.3	−2.9	1,141
Average	72	18.3	105.8	− 8.9	−2.2	$13,628 (total)
Standard & Poor's composite index	77	+16.1	104.7	− 8.3	+3.5	
DJIA	78	+ 2.9	83.0	−11.6	+8.7	

[a] These are the stock funds with the largest net assets at the end of 1970, but using only one fund from each management group. Data supplied by Wiesenberger Financial Services.

1969 and 1970. We also give average results based on the sum of one share of each of the ten funds. These companies had combined assets of over $15 billion at the end of 1969, or about one-third of all the common-stock funds. Thus they should be fairly representative of the industry as a whole. (In theory, there should be a bias in this list on the side of better than industry performance, since these better companies should have been entitled to more rapid expansion than the others; but this may not be the case in practice.)

Some interesting facts can be gathered from this table. First, we find that the overall results of these ten funds for 1961–1970 were not appreciably different from those of the Standard & Poor's 500-stock composite average (or the S & P 425-industrial stock average). But they were definitely better than those of the DJIA. (This raises the intriguing question as to why the 30 giants in the DJIA did worse than the much more numerous and apparently rather miscellaneous list used by Standard & Poor's.)* A second point is that the funds' aggregate performance as against the S & P index has improved somewhat in the last five years, compared with the preceding five. The funds' gain ran a little lower than S & P's in 1961–1965 and a little higher than S & P's in 1966–1970. The third point is that a wide difference exists between the results of the individual funds.

We do not think the mutual-fund industry can be criticized for doing no better than the market as a whole. Their managers and their professional competitors administer so large a portion of all marketable common stocks that what happens to the market as a whole must necessarily happen (approximately) to the sum of their funds. (Note that the trust assets of insured commercial banks included $181 billion of common stocks at the end of 1969; if we add to this the common stocks in accounts handled by investment advisers, plus the $56 billion of mutual and similar funds, we must conclude that the combined decisions of these professionals pretty well determine the movements of the stock averages, and that the

---

* For periods as long as 10 years, the returns of the Dow and the S & P 500 can diverge by fairly wide margins. Over the course of the typical investing lifetime, however—say 25 to 50 years—their returns have tended to converge quite closely.

movement of the stock averages pretty well determines the funds' aggregate results.)

Are there better than average funds and can the investor select these so as to obtain superior results for himself? Obviously all investors could not do this, since in that case we would soon be back where we started, with no one doing better than anyone else. Let us consider the question first in a simplified fashion. Why shouldn't the investor find out what fund has made the best showing of the lot over a period of sufficient years in the past, assume from this that its management is the most capable and will therefore do better than average in the future, and put his money in that fund? This idea appears the more practicable because, in the case of the mutual funds, he could obtain this "most capable management" without paying any special premium for it as against the other funds. (By contrast, among noninvestment corporations the best-managed companies sell at correspondingly high prices in relation to their current earnings and assets.)

The evidence on this point has been conflicting over the years. But our Table 9-1 covering the ten largest funds indicates that the results shown by the top five performers of 1961–1965 carried over *on the whole* through 1966–1970, even though two of this set did not do as well as two of the other five. Our studies indicate that the investor in mutual-fund shares may properly consider comparative performance over a period of years in the past, say at least five, *provided* the data do not represent a large net upward movement of the market as a whole. In the latter case spectacularly favorable results may be achieved in unorthodox ways—as will be demonstrated in our following section on "performance" funds. Such results in themselves may indicate only that the fund managers are taking undue speculative risks, and getting away with same *for the time being*.

"Performance" Funds

One of the new phenomena of recent years was the appearance of the cult of "performance" in the management of investment funds (and even of many trust funds). We must start this section with the important disclaimer that it does not apply to the large majority of well-established funds, but only to a relatively small section of the industry which has attracted a disproportionate amount of attention. The story is simple enough. Some of those in charge set out to get much better than average (or DJIA) results. They succeeded in doing this for a while, garnering considerable publicity and additional funds to manage. The aim was legitimate enough; unfortunately, it appears that, in the context of investing really sizable funds, the aim cannot be accomplished without incurring sizable risks. And in a comparatively short time the risks came home to roost.

Several of the circumstances surrounding the "performance" phenomenon caused ominous headshaking by those of us whose experience went far back—even to the 1920s—and whose views, for that very reason, were considered old-fashioned and irrelevant to this (second) "New Era." In the first place, and on this very point, nearly all these brilliant performers were young men—in their thirties and forties—whose direct financial experience was limited to the all but continuous bull market of 1948–1968. Secondly, they often acted as if the definition of a "sound investment" was a stock that was likely to have a good rise in the market in the next few months. This led to large commitments in newer ventures at prices completely disproportionate to their assets or recorded earnings. They could be "justified" only by a combination of naïve hope in the future accomplishments of these enterprises with an apparent shrewdness in exploiting the speculative enthusiasms of the uninformed and greedy public.

This section will not mention people's names. But we have every reason to give concrete examples of companies. The "performance fund" most in the public's eye was undoubtedly Manhattan Fund, Inc., organized at the end of 1965. Its first offering was of 27 million shares at $9.25 to $10 per share. The company started out with $247 million of capital. Its emphasis was, of course, on capital gains. Most of its funds were invested in issues selling at high multipliers of current earnings, paying no dividends (or very small ones), with a large speculative following and spectacular price movements. The fund showed an overall gain of 38.6% in 1967, against 11% for the S & P composite index. But thereafter its performance left much to be desired, as is shown in Table 9-2.

TABLE 9-2   A Performance-Fund Portfolio and Performance
(Larger Holdings of Manhattan Fund, December 31, 1969)

Shares Held (thousands)	Issue	Price	Earned 1969	Dividend 1969	Market Value (millions)
60	Teleprompter	99	$ .99	none	$ 6.0
190	Deltona	60½	2.32	none	11.5
280	Fedders	34	1.28	$ .35	9.5
105	Horizon Corp.	53½	2.68	none	5.6
150	Rouse Co.	34	.07	none	5.1
130	Mattel Inc.	64¼	1.11	.20	8.4
120	Polaroid	125	1.90	.32	15.0
244[a]	Nat'l Student Mkt'g	28½	.32	none	6.1
56	Telex Corp.	90½	.68	none	5.0
100	Bausch & Lomb	77¾	1.92	.80	7.8
190	Four Seasons Nursing	66	.80	none	12.3[b]
20	Int. Bus. Machines	365	8.21	3.60	7.3
41.5	Nat'l Cash Register	160	1.95	1.20	6.7
100	Saxon Ind.	109	3.81	none	10.9
105	Career Academy	50	.43	none	5.3
285	King Resources	28	.69	none	8.1
					$130.6
				Other common stocks	93.8
				Other holdings	19.6
				Total investments[c]	$244.0

[a] After 2-for-1 split.

[b] Also $1.1 million of affiliated stocks.

[c] Excluding cash equivalents.

Annual Performance Compared with S & P Composite Index

	1966	1967	1968	1969	1970	1971
Manhattan Fund	− 6 %	+38.6%	− 7.3%	−13.3%	−36.9%	+ 9.6%
S & P Composite	−10.1%	+23.0%	+10.4%	− 8.3%	+ 3.5%	+13.5%

The portfolio of Manhattan Fund at the end of 1969 was unorthodox to say the least. It is an extraordinary fact that two of its largest investments were in companies that filed for bankruptcy within six months thereafter, and a third faced creditors' actions in 1971. It is another extraordinary fact that shares of at least one of these doomed companies were bought not only by investment funds but by university endowment funds, the trust departments of large banking institutions, and the like.* A third extraordinary fact was that the founder-manager of Manhattan Fund sold his stock in a separately organized management company to another large concern for over $20 million in its stock; at that time the management company sold had less than $1 million in assets. This is undoubtedly one of the greatest disparities of all times between the results for the "manager" and the "managees."

A book published at the end of 1969[2] provided profiles of nineteen men "who are tops at the demanding game of managing billions of dollars of other people's money." The summary told us further that "they are young . . . some earn more than a million dollars a year . . . they are a new financial breed . . . they all have a total fascination with the market . . . and a spectacular knack for coming up with winners." A fairly good idea of the accomplishments of this top group can be obtained by examining the published results of the funds they manage. Such results are available for funds directed by twelve of the nineteen persons described in *The Money Managers.* Typically enough, they showed up well in 1966, and brilliantly in 1967. In 1968 their performance was still good in the aggregate, but mixed as to individual funds. In 1969 they all showed losses, with only one managing to do a bit better than the S & P composite index. In 1970 their comparative performance was even worse than in 1969.

---

* One of the "doomed companies" Graham refers to was National Student Marketing Corp., a con game masquerading as a stock, whose saga was told brilliantly in Andrew Tobias's *The Funny Money Game* (Playboy Press, New York, 1971). Among the supposedly sophisticated investors who were snookered by NSM's charismatic founder, Cort Randell, were the endowment funds of Cornell and Harvard and the trust departments at such prestigious banks as Morgan Guaranty and Bankers Trust.

We have presented this picture in order to point a moral, which perhaps can best be expressed by the old French proverb: *Plus ça change, plus c'est la même chose.* Bright, energetic people—usually quite young—have promised to perform miracles with "other people's money" since time immemorial. They have usually been able to do it for a while—or at least to appear to have done it—and they have inevitably brought losses to their public in the end.* About a half century ago the "miracles" were often accompanied by flagrant manipulation, misleading corporate reporting, outrageous capitalization structures, and other semifraudulent financial practices. All this brought on an elaborate system of financial controls by the SEC, as well as a cautious attitude toward common stocks on the part of the general public. The operations of the new "money managers" in 1965–1969 came a little more than one full generation after the shenanigans of 1926–1929.† The specific malpractices banned after the 1929 crash were no longer resorted to—they involved the risk of jail sentences. But in many corners of Wall Street they were replaced by newer gadgets and gimmicks that produced very similar results in the end. Outright manipulation of prices disappeared, but there were many other methods of drawing the gullible public's attention to the profit possibilities in "hot" issues. Blocks of "letter stock"[3] could be bought well below the quoted market price, subject to undisclosed restrictions on their sale; they could immediately be carried in the reports at their full market value, showing a lovely and illusory profit. And so on. It is

---

* As only the latest proof that "the more things change, the more they stay the same," consider that Ryan Jacob, a 29-year-old boy wonder, launched the Jacob Internet Fund at year-end 1999, after producing a 216% return at his previous dot-com fund. Investors poured nearly $300 million into Jacob's fund in the first few weeks of 2000. It then proceeded to lose 79.1% in 2000, 56.4% in 2001, and 13% in 2002—a cumulative collapse of 92%. That loss may have made Mr. Jacob's investors even older and wiser than it made him.

† Intriguingly, the disastrous boom and bust of 1999–2002 also came roughly 35 years after the previous cycle of insanity. Perhaps it takes about 35 years for the investors who remember the last "New Economy" craze to become less influential than those who do not. If this intuition is correct, the intelligent investor should be particularly vigilant around the year 2030.

amazing how, in a completely different atmosphere of regulation and prohibitions, Wall Street was able to duplicate so much of the excesses and errors of the 1920s.

No doubt there will be new regulations and new prohibitions. The specific abuses of the late 1960s will be fairly adequately banned from Wall Street. But it is probably too much to expect that the urge to speculate will ever disappear, or that the exploitation of that urge can ever be abolished. It is part of the armament of the intelligent investor to know about these "Extraordinary Popular Delusions,"[4] and to keep as far away from them as possible.

The picture of most of the performance funds is a poor one if we start *after* their spectacular record in 1967. With the 1967 figures included, their overall showing is not at all disastrous. On that basis one of "The Money Managers" operators did quite a bit better than the S & P composite index, three did distinctly worse, and six did about the same. Let us take as a check another group of performance funds—the ten that made the best showing in 1967, with gains ranging from 84% up to 301% in that single year. Of these, four gave a better overall four-year performance than the S & P index, if the 1967 gains are included; and two excelled the index in 1968–1970. None of these funds was large, and the average size was about $60 million. Thus, there is a strong indication that smaller size is a necessary factor for obtaining continued outstanding results.

The foregoing account contains the implicit conclusion that there may be special risks involved in looking for superior performance by investment-fund managers. All financial experience up to now indicates that large funds, soundly managed, can produce at best only slightly better than average results over the years. If they are unsoundly managed they can produce spectacular, but largely illusory, profits for a while, followed inevitably by calamitous losses. There have been instances of funds that have consistently outperformed the market averages for, say, ten years or more. But these have been scarce exceptions, having most of their operations in specialized fields, with self-imposed limits on the capital employed—and not actively sold to the public.*

---

* Today's equivalent of Graham's "scarce exceptions" tend to be open-end funds that are closed to new investors—meaning that the managers have

Closed-End versus Open-End Funds

Almost all the mutual funds or open-end funds, which offer their holders the right to cash in their shares at each day's valuation of the portfolio, have a corresponding machinery for selling new shares. By this means most of them have grown in size over the years. The closed-end companies, nearly all of which were organized a long time ago, have a fixed capital structure, and thus have diminished in relative dollar importance. Open-end companies are being sold by many thousands of energetic and persuasive salesmen, the closed-end shares have no one especially interested in distributing them. Consequently it has been possible to sell most "mutual funds" to the public at a fixed premium of about 9% above net asset value (to cover salesmen's commissions, etc.), while the majority of close-end shares have been consistently obtainable at *less* than their asset value. This price discount has varied among individual companies, and the average discount for the group as a whole has also varied from one date to another. Figures on this point for 1961–1970 are given in Table 9-3.

It does not take much shrewdness to suspect that the lower relative price for closed-end as against open-end shares has very little to do with the difference in the overall investment results between the two groups. That this is true is indicated by the comparison of the annual results for 1961–1970 of the two groups included in Table 9-3.

Thus we arrive at one of the few clearly evident rules for investors' choices. If you want to put money in investment funds, buy a group of closed-end shares at a discount of, say, 10% to 15% from asset value, instead of paying a premium of about 9% above asset value for shares of an open-end company. Assuming that the future dividends and changes in asset values continue to be about the same for the two groups, you will thus obtain about one-fifth more for your money from the closed-end shares.

The mutual-fund salesman will be quick to counter with the

---

stopped taking in any more cash. While that reduces the management fees they can earn, it maximizes the returns their existing shareholders can earn. Because most fund managers would rather look out for No. 1 than be No. 1, closing a fund to new investors is a rare and courageous step.

TABLE 9-3 Certain Data on Closed-End Funds, Mutual Funds, and S & P Composite Index

Year	*Average Discount of Closed-End Funds*	*Average Results of Closed-End Funds*[a]	*Average Results of Mutual Stock Funds*[b]	*Results of S & P Index*[c]
1970	− 6%	even	− 5.3%	+ 3.5%
1969		− 7.9%	−12.5	− 8.3
1968	(+ 7)[d]	+13.3	+15.4	+10.4
1967	− 5	+28.2	+37.2	+23.0
1966	−12	− 5.9	− 4.1	−10.1
1965	−14	+14.0	+24.8	+12.2
1964	−10	+16.9	+13.6	+14.8
1963	− 8	+20.8	+19.3	+24.0
1962	− 4	−11.6	−14.6	− 8.7
1961	− 3	+23.6	+25.7	+27.0
Average of 10 yearly figures:		+ 9.14%	+ 9.95%	+ 9.79%

[a] Wiesenberger average of ten diversified companies.

[b] Average of five Wiesenberger averages of common-stock funds each year.

[c] In all cases distributions are added back.

[d] Premium.

argument: "Ah, but if you own closed-end shares you can never be sure what price you can sell them for. The discount can be greater than it is today, and you will suffer from the wider spread. With our shares you are guaranteed the right to turn in your shares at 100% of asset value, never less." Let us examine this argument a bit; it will be a good exercise in logic and plain common sense. Question: Assuming that the discount on closed-end shares does widen, how likely is it that you will be worse off with those shares than with an otherwise equivalent purchase of open-end shares?

This calls for a little arithmetic. Assume that Investor A buys some open-end shares at 109% of asset value, and Investor B buys closed-end shares at 85% thereof, plus 1½% commission. Both sets of shares earn and pay 30% of this asset value in, say, four years,

TABLE 9-4   Average Results of Diversified Closed-End Funds, 1961–1970[a]

	1970	5 years, 1966–1970	1961–1970	Premium or Discount, December 1970
Three funds selling at premiums	−5.2%	+25.4%	+115.0%	11.4% premium
Ten funds selling at discounts	+1.3	+22.6	+102.9	9.2% discount

[a] Data from Wiesenberger Financial Services.

and end up with the same value as at the beginning. Investor A redeems his shares at 100% of value, losing the 9% premium he paid. His overall return for the period is 30% less 9%, or 21% on asset value. This, in turn, is 19% on his investment. How much must Investor B realize on his closed-end shares to obtain the same return on his investment as Investor A? The answer is 73%, or a discount of 27% from asset value. In other words, the closed-end man could suffer a widening of 12 points in the market discount (about double) before his return would get down to that of the open-end investor. An adverse change of this magnitude has happened rarely, if ever, in the history of closed-end shares. Hence it is very unlikely that you will obtain a lower overall return from a (representative) closed-end company, bought at a discount, if its investment performance is about equal to that of a representative mutual fund. If a small-load (or no-load) fund is substituted for one with the usual "8½%" load, the advantage of the closed-end investment is of course reduced, but it remains an advantage.

The fact that a few closed-end funds are selling at *premiums* greater than the true 9% charge on most mutual funds introduces a separate question for the investor. Do these premium companies enjoy superior management of sufficient proven worth to warrant their elevated prices? If the answer is sought in the comparative results for the past five or ten years, the answer would appear to be no. Three of the six premium companies have mainly foreign investments. A striking feature of these is the large variation in

TABLE 9-5   Comparison of Two Leading Closed-End Companies[a]

	1970	5 years, 1966–1970	10 years, 1961–1970	Premium or Discount, December 1970
General Am. Investors Co.	–0.3%	+34.0%	+165.6%	7.6% discount
Lehman Corp.	–7.2	+20.6	+108.0	13.9% premium

[a] Data from Wiesenberger Financial Services.

prices in a few years' time; at the end of 1970 one sold at only one-quarter of its high, another at a third, another at less than half. If we consider the three domestic companies selling above asset value, we find that the average of their ten-year overall returns was somewhat better than that of ten discount funds, but the opposite was true in the last five years. A comparison of the 1961–1970 record of Lehman Corp. and of General American Investors, two of our oldest and largest closed-end companies, is given in Table 9-5. One of these sold 14% above and the other 7.6% below its net-asset value at the end of 1970. The difference in price to net-asset relationships did not appear warranted by these figures.

Investment in Balanced Funds

The 23 balanced funds covered in the Wiesenberger Report had between 25% and 59% of their assets in preferred stocks and bonds, the average being just 40%. The balance was held in common stocks. It would appear more logical for the typical investor to make his bond-type investments directly, rather than to have them form part of a mutual-fund commitment. The average income return shown by these balanced funds in 1970 was only 3.9% per annum on asset value, or say 3.6% on the offering price. The better choice for the bond component would be the purchase of United States savings bonds, or corporate bonds rated A or better, or tax-free bonds, for the investor's bond portfolio.

COMMENTARY ON CHAPTER 9

The schoolteacher asks Billy Bob: "If you have twelve sheep and one jumps over the fence, how many sheep do you have left?"

Billy Bob answers, "None."

"Well," says the teacher, "you sure don't know your subtraction."

"Maybe not," Billy Bob replies, "but I darn sure know my sheep."

—an old Texas joke

ALMOST PERFECT

A purely American creation, the mutual fund was introduced in 1924 by a former salesman of aluminum pots and pans named Edward G. Leffler. Mutual funds are quite cheap, very convenient, generally diversified, professionally managed, and tightly regulated under some of the toughest provisions of Federal securities law. By making investing easy and affordable for almost anyone, the funds have brought some 54 million American families (and millions more around the world) into the investing mainstream—probably the greatest advance in financial democracy ever achieved.

But mutual funds aren't perfect; they are *almost* perfect, and that word makes all the difference. Because of their imperfections, most funds underperform the market, overcharge their investors, create tax headaches, and suffer erratic swings in performance. The intelligent investor must choose funds with great care in order to avoid ending up owning a big fat mess.

TOP OF THE CHARTS

Most investors simply buy a fund that has been going up fast, on the assumption that it will keep on going. And why not? Psychologists have shown that humans have an inborn tendency to believe that the long run can be predicted from even a short series of outcomes. What's more, we know from our own experience that some plumbers are far better than others, that some baseball players are much more likely to hit home runs, that our favorite restaurant serves consistently superior food, and that smart kids get consistently good grades. Skill and brains and hard work are recognized, rewarded—and consistently repeated—all around us. So, if a fund beats the market, our intuition tells us to expect it to keep right on outperforming.

Unfortunately, in the financial markets, luck is more important than skill. If a manager happens to be in the right corner of the market at just the right time, he will look brilliant—but all too often, what was hot suddenly goes cold and the manager's IQ seems to shrivel by 50 points. Figure 9-1 shows what happened to the hottest funds of 1999.

This is yet another reminder that the market's hottest market sector—in 1999, that was technology—often turns as cold as liquid nitrogen, with blinding speed and utterly no warning.[1] And it's a reminder that buying funds based purely on their past performance is one of the stupidest things an investor can do. Financial scholars have been studying mutual-fund performance for at least a half century, and they are virtually unanimous on several points:

- the average fund does not pick stocks well enough to overcome its costs of researching and trading them;
- the higher a fund's expenses, the lower its returns;
- the more frequently a fund trades its stocks, the less it tends to earn;

---

[1] Sector funds specializing in almost every imaginable industry are available—and date back to the 1920s. After nearly 80 years of history, the evidence is overwhelming: The most lucrative, and thus most popular, sector of any given year often turns out to be among the worst performers of the following year. Just as idle hands are the devil's workshop, sector funds are the investor's nemesis.

FIGURE 9-1   The Crash-and-Burn Club

Fund	Total Return				Value on 12/31/02 of $10,000 invested on 1/1/1999
	1999	2000	2001	2002	
Van Wagoner Emerging Growth	291.2	−20.9	−59.7	−64.6	4,419
Monument Internet	273.1	−56.9	−52.2	−51.2	3,756
Amerindo Technology	248.9	−64.8	−50.8	−31.0	4,175
PBHG Technology & Communications	243.9	−43.7	−52.4	−54.5	4,198
Van Wagoner Post-Venture	237.2	−30.3	−62.1	−67.3	2,907
ProFunds Ultra OTC	233.2	−73.7	−69.1	−69.4	829
Van Wagoner Technology	223.8	−28.1	−61.9	−65.8	3,029
Thurlow Growth	213.2	−56.0	−26.1	−31.0	7,015
Firsthand Technology Innovators	212.3	−37.9	−29.1	−54.8	6,217
Janus Global Technology	211.6	−33.7	−40.0	−40.9	7,327
Wilshire 5000 index (total stock market)	23.8	−10.9	−11.0	−20.8	7,780

Source: Lipper

Note: Monument Internet was later renamed Orbitex Emerging Technology.

These 10 funds were among the hottest performers of 1999—and, in fact, among the highest annual performers of all time. But the next three years erased all the giant gains of 1999, and then some.

- highly volatile funds, which bounce up and down more than average, are likely to stay volatile;
- funds with high past returns are unlikely to remain winners for long.[2]

Your chances of selecting the top-performing funds of the future on the basis of their returns in the past are about as high as the odds that Bigfoot and the Abominable Snowman will both show up in pink ballet slippers at your next cocktail party. In other words, your chances are not zero—but they're pretty close. (See sidebar, p. 255.)

But there's good news, too. First of all, understanding why it's so hard to find a good fund will help you become a more intelligent investor. Second, while past performance is a poor predictor of future returns, there are other factors that you can use to increase your odds of finding a good fund. Finally, a fund can offer excellent value even if it doesn't beat the market—by providing an economical way to diversify your holdings and by freeing up your time for all the other things you would rather be doing than picking your own stocks.

THE FIRST SHALL BE LAST

Why don't more winning funds stay winners?

The better a fund performs, the more obstacles its investors face:

Migrating managers. When a stock picker seems to have the Midas touch, everyone wants him—including rival fund companies. If you bought Transamerica Premier Equity Fund to cash in on the skills of Glen Bickerstaff, who gained 47.5% in 1997, you were quickly out of luck; TCW snatched him away in mid-1998 to run its TCW Galileo Select Equities Fund, and the Transamerica fund lagged the market in three of the next four years. If you bought Fidelity Aggressive Growth Fund in early 2000 to capitalize on the high returns of Erin Sullivan, who had nearly tripled her shareholders' money since 1997, oh well: She quit to start her own hedge fund in

---

[2] The research on mutual fund performance is too voluminous to cite. Useful summaries and links can be found at: www.investorhome.com/mutual.htm#do, www.ssrn.com (enter "mutual fund" in the search window), and www.stanford.edu/~wfsharpe/art/art.htm.

2000, and her former fund lost more than three-quarters of its value over the next three years.[3]

Asset elephantiasis. When a fund earns high returns, investors notice—often pouring in hundreds of millions of dollars in a matter of weeks. That leaves the fund manager with few choices—all of them bad. He can keep that money safe for a rainy day, but then the low returns on cash will crimp the fund's results if stocks keep going up. He can put the new money into the stocks he already owns—which have probably gone up since he first bought them and will become dangerously overvalued if he pumps in millions of dollars more. Or he can buy new stocks he didn't like well enough to own already—but he will have to research them from scratch and keep an eye on far more companies than he is used to following.

Finally, when the $100-million Nimble Fund puts 2% of its assets (or $2 million) in Minnow Corp., a stock with a total market value of $500 million, it's buying up less than one-half of 1% of Minnow. But if hot performance swells the Nimble Fund to $10 billion, then an investment of 2% of its assets would total $200 million—nearly half the entire value of Minnow, a level of ownership that isn't even permissible under Federal law. If Nimble's portfolio manager still wants to own small stocks, he will have to spread his money over vastly more companies—and probably end up spreading his attention too thin.

No more fancy footwork. Some companies specialize in "incubating" their funds—test-driving them privately before selling them publicly. (Typically, the only shareholders are employees and affiliates of the fund company itself.) By keeping them tiny, the sponsor can use these incubated funds as guinea pigs for risky strategies that work best with small sums of money, like buying truly tiny stocks or rapid-fire trading of initial public offerings. If its strategy succeeds, the fund can lure public investors en masse by publicizing its private returns. In other cases, the fund manager "waives" (or skips charging) management fees, raising the net return—then slaps the fees on later after the high returns attract plenty of customers. Almost without exception, the returns of incubated and fee-waived funds have faded into mediocrity after outside investors poured millions of dollars into them.

---

[3] That's not to say that these funds would have done better if their "superstar" managers had stayed in place; all we can be sure of is that the two funds did poorly without them.

Rising expenses. It often costs more to trade stocks in very large blocks than in small ones; with fewer buyers and sellers, it's harder to make a match. A fund with $100 million in assets might pay 1% a year in trading costs. But, if high returns send the fund mushrooming up to $10 billion, its trades could easily eat up at least 2% of those assets. The typical fund holds on to its stocks for only 11 months at a time, so trading costs eat away at returns like a corrosive acid. Meanwhile, the other costs of running a fund rarely fall—and sometimes even rise—as assets grow. With operating expenses averaging 1.5%, and trading costs at around 2%, the typical fund has to beat the market by 3.5 percentage points per year before costs just to match it after costs!

Sheepish behavior. Finally, once a fund becomes successful, its managers tend to become timid and imitative. As a fund grows, its fees become more lucrative—making its managers reluctant to rock the boat. The very risks that the managers took to generate their initial high returns could now drive investors away—and jeopardize all that fat fee income. So the biggest funds resemble a herd of identical and overfed sheep, all moving in sluggish lockstep, all saying "baaaa" at the same time. Nearly every growth fund owns Cisco and GE and Microsoft and Pfizer and Wal-Mart—and in almost identical proportions. This behavior is so prevalent that finance scholars simply call it herding.[4] But by protecting their own fee income, fund managers compromise their ability to produce superior returns for their outside investors.

---

[4] There's a second lesson here: To succeed, the individual investor must either avoid shopping from the same list of favorite stocks that have already been picked over by the giant institutions, or own them far more patiently. See Erik R. Sirri and Peter Tufano, "Costly Search and Mutual Fund Flows," *The Journal of Finance,* vol. 53, no. 8, October, 1998, pp. 1589–1622; Keith C. Brown, W. V. Harlow, and Laura Starks, "Of Tournaments and Temptations," *The Journal of Finance,* vol. 51, no. 1, March, 1996, pp. 85–110; Josef Lakonishok, Andrei Shleifer, and Robert Vishny, "What Do Money Managers Do?" working paper, University of Illinois, February, 1997; Stanley Eakins, Stanley Stansell, and Paul Wertheim, "Institutional Portfolio Composition," *Quarterly Review of Economics and Finance,* vol. 38, no. 1, Spring, 1998, pp. 93–110; Paul Gompers and Andrew Metrick, "Institutional Investors and Equity Prices," *The Quarterly Journal of Economics,* vol. 116, no. 1, February, 2001, pp. 229–260.

FIGURE 9-2 The Funnel of Fund Performance

Looking back from December 31, 2002, how many U.S. stock funds outperformed Vanguard 500 Index Fund?

One year:
1,186 of 2,423 funds (or 48.9%)

Three years:
1,157 of 1,944 funds (or 59.5%)

Five years:
768 of 1,494 funds (or 51.4%)

Ten years:
227 of 728 funds (or 31.2%)

Fifteen years:
125 of 445 funds (or 28.1%)

Twenty years:
37 of 248 funds (or 14.9%)

Source: Lipper Inc.

Because of their fat costs and bad behavior, most funds fail to earn their keep. No wonder high returns are nearly as perishable as unrefrigerated fish. What's more, as time passes, the drag of their excessive expenses leaves most funds farther and farther behind, as Figure 9.2 shows.[5]

What, then, should the intelligent investor do?

First of all, recognize that an index fund—which owns all the stocks

---

[5] Amazingly, this illustration *understates* the advantage of index funds, since the database from which it is taken does not include the track records of hundreds of funds that disappeared over these periods. Measured more accurately, the advantage of indexing would be overpowering.

in the market, all the time, without any pretense of being able to select the "best" and avoid the "worst"—will beat most funds over the long run. (If your company doesn't offer a low-cost index fund in your 401(k), organize your coworkers and petition to have one added.) Its rock-bottom overhead—operating expenses of 0.2% annually, and yearly trading costs of just 0.1%—give the index fund an insurmountable advantage. If stocks generate, say, a 7% annualized return over the next 20 years, a low-cost index fund like Vanguard Total Stock Market will return just under 6.7%. (That would turn a $10,000 investment into more than $36,000.) But the average stock fund, with its 1.5% in operating expenses and roughly 2% in trading costs, will be lucky to gain 3.5% annually. (That would turn $10,000 into just under $20,000—or *nearly 50% less* than the result from the index fund.)

Index funds have only one significant flaw: They are boring. You'll never be able to go to a barbecue and brag about how you own the top-performing fund in the country. You'll never be able to boast that you beat the market, because the job of an index fund is to match the market's return, not to exceed it. Your index-fund manager is not likely to "roll the dice" and gamble that the next great industry will be teleportation, or scratch-'n'-sniff websites, or telepathic weight-loss clinics; the fund will always own every stock, not just one manager's best guess at the next new thing. But, as the years pass, the cost advantage of indexing will keep accruing relentlessly. Hold an index fund for 20 years or more, adding new money every month, and you are all but certain to outperform the vast majority of professional and individual investors alike. Late in his life, Graham praised index funds as the best choice for individual investors, as does Warren Buffett.[6]

---

[6] See Benjamin Graham, *Benjamin Graham: Memoirs of the Dean of Wall Street,* Seymour Chatman, ed. (McGraw-Hill, New York, 1996), p. 273, and Janet Lowe, *The Rediscovered Benjamin Graham: Selected Writings of the Wall Street Legend* (John Wiley & Sons, New York, 1999), p. 273. As Warren Buffett wrote in his 1996 annual report: "Most investors, both institutional and individual, will find that the best way to own common stocks is through an index fund that charges minimal fees. Those following this path are sure to beat the net results (after fees and expenses) delivered by the great majority of investment professionals." (See www.berkshirehathaway. com/1996ar/1996.html.)

TILTING THE TABLES

When you add up all their handicaps, the wonder is not that so few funds beat the index, but that any do. And yet, some do. What qualities do they have in common?

Their managers are the biggest shareholders. The conflict of interest between what's best for the fund's managers and what's best for its investors is mitigated when the managers are among the biggest owners of the fund's shares. Some firms, like Longleaf Partners, even forbid their employees from owning anything but their own funds. At Longleaf and other firms like Davis and FPA, the managers own so much of the funds that they are likely to manage your money as if it were their own—lowering the odds that they will jack up fees, let the funds swell to gargantuan size, or whack you with a nasty tax bill. A fund's proxy statement and Statement of Additional Information, both available from the Securities and Exchange Commission through the EDGAR database at www.sec.gov, disclose whether the managers own at least 1% of the fund's shares.

They are cheap. One of the most common myths in the fund business is that "you get what you pay for"—that high returns are the best justification for higher fees. There are two problems with this argument. First, it isn't true; decades of research have proven that funds with higher fees earn *lower* returns over time. Secondly, high returns are temporary, while high fees are nearly as permanent as granite. If you buy a fund for its hot returns, you may well end up with a handful of cold ashes—but your costs of owning the fund are almost certain *not* to decline when its returns do.

They dare to be different. When Peter Lynch ran Fidelity Magellan, he bought whatever seemed cheap to him—regardless of what other fund managers owned. In 1982, his biggest investment was Treasury bonds; right after that, he made Chrysler his top holding, even though most experts expected the automaker to go bankrupt; then, in 1986, Lynch put almost 20% of Fidelity Magellan in foreign stocks like Honda, Norsk Hydro, and Volvo. So, before you buy a U.S. stock fund, compare the holdings listed in its latest report against the roster of the S & P 500 index; if they look like Tweedledee and Tweedledum, shop for another fund.[7]

---

[7] A complete listing of the S & P 500's constituent companies is available at www.standardandpoors.com.

They shut the door. The best funds often close to new investors—permitting only their existing shareholders to buy more. That stops the feeding frenzy of new buyers who want to pile in at the top and protects the fund from the pains of asset elephantiasis. It's also a signal that the fund managers are not putting their own wallets ahead of yours. But the closing should occur before—not after—the fund explodes in size. Some companies with an exemplary record of shutting their own gates are Longleaf, Numeric, Oakmark, T. Rowe Price, Vanguard, and Wasatch.

They don't advertise. Just as Plato says in *The Republic* that the ideal rulers are those who do not want to govern, the best fund managers often behave as if they don't want your money. They don't appear constantly on financial television or run ads boasting of their No. 1 returns. The steady little Mairs & Power Growth Fund didn't even have a website until 2001 and still sells its shares in only 24 states. The Torray Fund has never run a retail advertisement since its launch in 1990.

What else should you watch for? Most fund buyers look at past performance first, then at the manager's reputation, then at the riskiness of the fund, and finally (if ever) at the fund's expenses.[8]

The intelligent investor looks at those same things—but in the opposite order.

Since a fund's expenses are far more predictable than its future risk or return, you should make them your first filter. There's no good reason ever to pay more than these levels of annual operating expenses, by fund category:

- Taxable and municipal bonds: 0.75%
- U.S. equities (large and mid-sized stocks): 1.0%
- High-yield (junk) bonds: 1.0%

---

[8] See Noel Capon, Gavan Fitzsimons, and Russ Alan Prince, "An Individual Level Analysis of the Mutual Fund Investment Decision," *Journal of Financial Services Research,* vol. 10, 1996, pp. 59–82; Investment Company Institute, "Understanding Shareholders' Use of Information and Advisers," Spring, 1997, at www.ici.org/pdf/rpt_undstnd_share.pdf, p. 21; Gordon Alexander, Jonathan Jones, and Peter Nigro, "Mutual Fund Shareholders: Characteristics, Investor Knowledge, and Sources of Information," OCC working paper, December, 1997, at www.occ.treas.gov/ftp/workpaper/wp97-13.pdf.

- U.S. equities (small stocks):   1.25%
- Foreign stocks: 1.50%[9]

Next, evaluate risk. In its prospectus (or buyer's guide), every fund must show a bar graph displaying its worst loss over a calendar quarter. If you can't stand losing at least that much money in three months, go elsewhere. It's also worth checking a fund's Morningstar rating. A leading investment research firm, Morningstar awards "star ratings" to funds, based on how much risk they took to earn their returns (one star is the worst, five is the best). But, just like past performance itself, these ratings look back in time; they tell you which funds were the best, not which are going to be. Five-star funds, in fact, have a disconcerting habit of going on to underperform one-star funds. So first find a low-cost fund whose managers are major shareholders, dare to be different, don't hype their returns, and have shown a willingness to shut down before they get too big for their britches. Then, and only then, consult their Morningstar rating.[10]

Finally, look at past performance, remembering that it is only a pale predictor of future returns. As we've already seen, yesterday's winners often become tomorrow's losers. But researchers have shown that one thing is almost certain: Yesterday's losers almost never become tomorrow's winners. So avoid funds with consistently poor past returns—especially if they have above-average annual expenses.

THE CLOSED WORLD OF CLOSED-END FUNDS

Closed-end stock funds, although popular during the 1980s, have slowly atrophied. Today, there are only 30 diversified domestic

---

[9] Investors can search easily for funds that meet these expense hurdles by using the fund-screening tools at www.morningstar.com and http://money.cnn.com.

[10] See Matthew Morey, "Rating the Raters: An Investigation of Mutual Fund Rating Services," *Journal of Investment Consulting,* vol. 5, no. 2, November/December, 2002. While its star ratings are a weak predictor of future results, Morningstar is the single best source of information on funds for individual investors.

equity funds, many of them tiny, trading only a few hundred shares a day, with high expenses and weird strategies (like Morgan Fun-Shares, which specializes in the stocks of "habit-forming" industries like booze, casinos, and cigarettes). Research by closed-end fund expert Donald Cassidy of Lipper Inc. reinforces Graham's earlier observations: Diversified closed-end stock funds trading at a discount not only tend to outperform those trading at a premium but are likely to have a better return than the average open-end mutual fund. Sadly, however, diversified closed-end stock funds are not always available at a discount in what has become a dusty, dwindling market.[11]

But there are hundreds of closed-end bond funds, with especially strong choices available in the municipal-bond area. When these funds trade at a discount, their yield is amplified and they can be attractive, so long as their annual expenses are below the thresholds listed above.[12]

The new breed of exchange-traded index funds can be worth exploring as well. These low-cost "ETFs" sometimes offer the only means by which an investor can gain entrée to a narrow market like, say, companies based in Belgium or stocks in the semiconductor industry. Other index ETFs offer much broader market exposure. However, they are generally not suitable for investors who wish to add money regularly, since most brokers will charge a separate commission on every new investment you make.[13]

---

[11] Unlike a mutual fund, a closed-end fund does not issue new shares directly to anyone who wants to buy them. Instead, an investor must buy shares not from the fund itself, but from another shareholder who is willing to part with them. Thus, the price of the shares fluctuates above and below their net asset value, depending on supply and demand.

[12] For more information, see www.morningstar.com and www.etfconnect.com.

[13] Unlike index mutual funds, index ETFs are subject to standard stock commissions when you buy and sell them—and these commissions are often assessed on any additional purchases or reinvested dividends. Details are available at www.ishares.com, www.streettracks.com, www.amex.com, and www.indexfunds.com.

KNOW WHEN TO FOLD 'EM

Once you own a fund, how can you tell when it's time to sell? The standard advice is to ditch a fund if it underperforms the market (or similar portfolios) for one—or is it two?—or is it three?—years in a row. But this advice makes no sense. From its birth in 1970 through 1999, the Sequoia Fund underperformed the S & P 500 index in 12 out of its 29 years—or more than 41% of the time. Yet Sequoia gained more than 12,500% over that period, versus 4,900% for the index.[14]

The performance of most funds falters simply because the type of stocks they prefer temporarily goes out of favor. If you hired a manager to invest in a particular way, why fire him for doing what he promised? By selling when a style of investing is out of fashion, you not only lock in a loss but lock yourself out of the all-but-inevitable recovery. One study showed that mutual-fund investors underperformed their own funds by 4.7 percentage points annually from 1998 through 2001— simply by buying high and selling low.[15]

So when should you sell? Here a few definite red flags:

- **a sharp and unexpected change in strategy**, such as a "value" fund loading up on technology stocks in 1999 or a "growth" fund buying tons of insurance stocks in 2002;
- **an increase in expenses**, suggesting that the managers are lining their own pockets;
- **large and frequent tax bills** generated by excessive trading;
- **suddenly erratic returns**, as when a formerly conservative fund generates a big loss (or even produces a giant gain).

---

[14] See Sequoia's June 30, 1999, report to shareholders at www.sequoia fund.com/Reports/Quarterly/SemiAnn99.htm. Sequoia has been closed to new investors since 1982, which has reinforced its superb performance.
[15] Jason Zweig, "What Fund Investors Really Need to Know," *Money*, June, 2002, pp. 110–115.

WHY WE LOVE OUR OUIJA BOARDS

Believing—or even just hoping—that we can pick the best funds of the future makes us feel better. It gives us the pleasing sensation that we are in charge of our own investment destiny. This "I'm-in-control-here" feeling is part of the human condition; it's what psychologists call overconfidence. Here are just a few examples of how it works:

- In 1999, *Money* Magazine asked more than 500 people whether their portfolios had beaten the market. One in four said yes. When asked to specify their returns, however, 80% of those investors reported gains *lower* than the market's. (Four percent had no idea how much their portfolios rose—but were sure they had beaten the market anyway!)
- A Swedish study asked drivers who had been in severe car crashes to rate their own skills behind the wheel. These people—including some the police had found responsible for the accidents and others who had been so badly injured that they answered the survey from their hospital beds—insisted they were better-than-average drivers.
- In a poll taken in late 2000, *Time* and CNN asked more than 1,000 likely voters whether they thought they were in the top 1% of the population by income. Nineteen percent placed themselves among the richest 1% of Americans.
- In late 1997, a survey of 750 investors found that 74% believed their mutual-fund holdings would "consistently beat the Standard & Poor's 500 each year"—even though most funds fail to beat the S & P 500 in the long run and many fail to beat it in *any* year.[1]

While this kind of optimism is a normal sign of a healthy psyche, that doesn't make it good investment policy. It makes sense to believe you can predict something only if it actually *is* predictable. Unless you are realistic, your quest for self-esteem will end up in self-defeat.

---

[1] See Jason Zweig, "Did You Beat the Market?" *Money,* January, 2000, pp. 55–58; *Time*/CNN poll #15, October 25–26, 2000, question 29.

As the investment consultant Charles Ellis puts it, "If you're not prepared to stay married, you shouldn't *get* married."[16] Fund investing is no different. If you're not prepared to stick with a fund through at least three lean years, you shouldn't buy it in the first place. Patience is the fund investor's single most powerful ally.

[16] See interview with Ellis in Jason Zweig, "Wall Street's Wisest Man," *Money*, June, 2001, pp. 49–52.

CHAPTER 10

The Investor and His Advisers

*T*he investment of money in securities is unique among business operations in that it is almost always based in some degree on advice received from others. The great bulk of investors are amateurs. Naturally they feel that in choosing their securities they can profit by professional guidance. Yet there are peculiarities inherent in the very concept of investment advice.

If the reason people invest is to make money, then in seeking advice they are asking others to tell them how to make money. That idea has some element of naïveté. Businessmen seek professional advice on various elements of their business, but they do not expect to be told how to make a profit. That is their own bailiwick. When they, or nonbusiness people, rely on others to make *investment profits* for them, they are expecting a kind of result for which there is no true counterpart in ordinary business affairs.

If we assume that there are normal or standard *income* results to be obtained from investing money in securities, then the role of the adviser can be more readily established. He will use his superior training and experience to protect his clients against mistakes and to make sure that they obtain the results to which their money is entitled. It is when the investor demands more than an average return on his money, or when his adviser undertakes to do better for him, that the question arises whether more is being asked or promised than is likely to be delivered.

Advice on investments may be obtained from a variety of sources. These include: (1) a relative or friend, presumably knowledgeable in securities; (2) a local (commercial) banker; (3) a brokerage firm or investment banking house; (4) a financial service or periodical; and (5) an investment counselor.* The miscellaneous character of this list suggests that no logical or systematic approach in this matter has crystallized, as yet, in the minds of investors.

Certain common-sense considerations relate to the criterion of normal or standard results mentioned above. Our basic thesis is this: If the investor is to rely chiefly on the advice of others in handling his funds, then either he must limit himself and his advisers strictly to standard, conservative, and even unimaginative forms of investment, or he must have an unusually intimate and favorable knowledge of the person who is going to direct his funds into other channels. But if the ordinary business or professional relationship exists between the investor and his advisers, he can be receptive to *less conventional* suggestions only to the extent that he himself has grown in knowledge and experience and has therefore become competent to pass independent judgment on the recommendations of others. He has then passed from the category of defensive or unenterprising investor into that of aggressive or enterprising investor.

Investment Counsel and Trust Services of Banks

The truly professional investment advisers—that is, the well-established investment counsel firms, who charge substantial annual fees—are quite modest in their promises and pretentions. For the most part they place their clients' funds in standard interest- and dividend-paying securities, and they rely mainly on normal investment experience for their overall results. In the typical case it is doubtful whether more than 10% of the total fund is ever invested in securities other than those of leading companies, plus

---

* The list of sources for investment advice remains as "miscellaneous" as it was when Graham wrote. A survey of investors conducted in late 2002 for the Securities Industry Association, a Wall Street trade group, found that 17% of investors depended most heavily for investment advice on a spouse or friend; 2% on a banker; 16% on a broker; 10% on financial periodicals; and 24% on a financial planner. The only difference from Graham's day is that 8% of investors now rely heavily on the Internet and 3% on financial television. (See www.sia.com.)

government bonds (including state and municipal issues); nor do they make a serious effort to take advantage of swings in the general market.

The leading investment-counsel firms make no claim to being brilliant; they do pride themselves on being careful, conservative, and competent. Their primary aim is to conserve the principal value over the years and produce a conservatively acceptable rate of income. Any accomplishment beyond that—and they do strive to better the goal—they regard in the nature of extra service rendered. Perhaps their chief value to their clients lies in shielding them from costly mistakes. They offer as much as the defensive investor has the right to expect from any counselor serving the general public.

What we have said about the well-established investment-counsel firms applies generally to the trust and advisory services of the larger banks.*

Financial Services

The so-called financial services are organizations that send out uniform bulletins (sometimes in the form of telegrams) to their subscribers. The subjects covered may include the state and prospects of business, the behavior and prospect of the securities markets, and information and advice regarding individual issues. There is often an "inquiry department" which will answer questons affecting an individual subscriber. The cost of the service averages much less than the fee that investment counselors charge their individual clients. Some organizations—notably Babson's and Standard & Poor's—operate on separate levels as a financial service and as investment counsel. (Incidentally, other organiza-

---

* The character of investment counseling firms and trust banks has not changed, but today they generally do not offer their services to investors with less than $1 million in financial assets; in some cases, $5 million or more is required. Today thousands of independent financial-planning firms perform very similar functions, although (as analyst Robert Veres puts it) the mutual fund has replaced blue-chip stocks as the investment of choice and diversification has replaced "quality" as the standard of safety.

tions—such as Scudder, Stevens & Clark—operate separately as investment counsel and as one or more investment funds.)

The financial services direct themselves, on the whole, to a quite different segment of the public than do the investment-counsel firms. The latters' clients generally wish to be relieved of bother and the need for making decisions. The financial services offer information and guidance to those who are directing their own financial affairs or are themselves advising others. Many of these services confine themselves exclusively, or nearly so, to forecasting market movements by various "technical" methods. We shall dismiss these with the observation that their work does not concern "investors" as the term is used in this book.

On the other hand, some of the best known—such as Moody's Investment Service and Standard & Poor's—are identified with statistical organizations that compile the voluminous statistical data that form the basis for all serious security analysis. These services have a varied clientele, ranging from the most conservative-minded investor to the rankest speculator. As a result they must find it difficult to adhere to any clear-cut or fundamental philosophy in arriving at their opinions and recommendations.

An old-established service of the type of Moody's and the others must obviously provide something worthwhile to a broad class of investors. What is it? Basically they address themselves to the matters in which the average active investor-speculator is interested, and their views on these either command some measure of authority or at least appear more reliable than those of the unaided client.

For years the financial services have been making stock-market forecasts without anyone taking this activity very seriously. Like everyone else in the field they are sometimes right and sometimes wrong. Wherever possible they hedge their opinions so as to avoid the risk of being proved completely wrong. (There is a well-developed art of Delphic phrasing that adjusts itself successfully to whatever the future brings.) In our view—perhaps a prejudiced one—this segment of their work has no real significance except for the light it throws on human nature in the securities markets. Nearly everyone interested in common stocks wants to be told by someone else what he thinks the market is going to do. The demand being there, it must be supplied.

Their interpretations and forecasts of business conditions, of course, are much more authoritative and informing. These are an important part of the great body of economic intelligence which is spread continuously among buyers and sellers of securities and tends to create fairly rational prices for stocks and bonds under most circumstances. Undoubtedly the material published by the financial services adds to the store of information available and fortifies the investment judgment of their clients.

It is difficult to evaluate their recommendations of individual securities. Each service is entitled to be judged separately, and the verdict could properly be based only on an elaborate and inclusive study covering many years. In our own experience we have noted among them a pervasive attitude which we think tends to impair what could otherwise be more useful advisory work. This is their general view that a stock should be bought if the near-term prospects of the business are favorable and should be sold if these are unfavorable—*regardless of the current price.* Such a superficial principle often prevents the services from doing the sound analytical job of which their staffs are capable—namely, to ascertain whether a given stock appears over- or undervalued at the current price in the light of its indicated long-term future earning power.

The intelligent investor will not do his buying and selling solely on the basis of recommendations received from a financial service. Once this point is established, the role of the financial service then becomes the useful one of supplying information and offering suggestions.

Advice from Brokerage Houses

Probably the largest volume of information and advice to the security-owning public comes from stockbrokers. These are members of the New York Stock Exchange, and of other exchanges, who execute buying and selling orders for a standard commission. Practically all the houses that deal with the public maintain a "statistical" or analytical department, which answers inquiries and makes recommendations. A great deal of analytical literature, some of it elaborate and expensive, is distributed gratis to the firms' customers—more impressively referred to as clients.

A great deal is at stake in the innocent-appearing question whether "customers" or "clients" is the more appropriate name. A business has customers; a professional person or organization has clients. The Wall Street brokerage fraternity has probably the high-est ethical standards of any *business*, but it is still feeling its way toward the standards and standing of a true profession.*

In the past Wall Street has thrived mainly on speculation, and stock-market speculators as a class were almost certain to lose money. Hence it has been logically impossible for brokerage houses to operate on a thoroughly professional basis. To do that would have required them to direct their efforts toward reducing rather than increasing their business.

The farthest that certain brokerage houses have gone in that direction—and could have been expected to go—is to refrain from inducing or encouraging anyone to speculate. Such houses have confined themselves to executing orders given them, to supplying financial information and analyses, and to rendering opinions on the investment merits of securities. Thus, in theory at least, they are devoid of all responsibility for either the profits or the losses of their speculative customers.†

Most stock-exchange houses, however, still adhere to the old-time slogans that they are in business to make commissions and that the way to succeed in business is to give the customers what they want. Since the most profitable customers want speculative advice and suggestions, the thinking and activities of the typical firm are pretty closely geared to day-to-day trading in the market. Thus it tries hard to help its customers make money in a field where they are condemned almost by mathematical law to lose in the end.‡ By this we mean that the speculative part of their opera-tions cannot be profitable over the long run for most brokerage-

---

* Overall, Graham was as tough and cynical an observer as Wall Street has ever seen. In this rare case, however, he was not nearly cynical enough. Wall Street may have higher ethical standards than *some* businesses (smug-gling, prostitution, Congressional lobbying, and journalism come to mind) but the investment world nevertheless has enough liars, cheaters, and thieves to keep Satan's check-in clerks frantically busy for decades to come.
† The thousands of people who bought stocks in the late 1990s in the belief that Wall Street analysts were providing unbiased and valuable advice have learned, in a painful way, how right Graham is on this point.
‡ Interestingly, this stinging criticism, which in his day Graham was directing at full-service brokers, ended up applying to discount Internet brokers in the

house customers. But to the extent that their operations resemble true investing they may produce investment gains that more than offset the speculative losses.

The investor obtains advice and information from stock-exchange houses through two types of employees, now known officially as "customers' brokers" (or "account executives") and financial analysts.

The customer's broker, also called a "registered representative," formerly bore the less dignified title of "customer's man." Today he is for the most part an individual of good character and considerable knowledge of securities, who operates under a rigid code of right conduct. Nevertheless, since his business is to earn commissions, he can hardly avoid being speculation-minded. Thus the security buyer who wants to avoid being influenced by speculative considerations will ordinarily have to be careful and explicit in his dealing with his customer's broker; he will have to show clearly, by word and deed, that he is not interested in anything faintly resembling a stock-market "tip." Once the customer's broker understands clearly that he has a real investor on his hands, he will respect this point of view and cooperate with it.

The financial analyst, formerly known chiefly as security analyst, is a person of particular concern to the author, who has been one himself for more than five decades and has helped educate countless others. At this stage we refer only to the financial analysts employed by brokerage houses. The function of the security analyst is clear enough from his title. It is he who works up the detailed studies of individual securities, develops careful comparisons of various issues in the same field, and forms an expert opinion of the safety or attractiveness or intrinsic value of all the different kinds of stocks and bonds.

---

late 1990s. These firms spent millions of dollars on flashy advertising that goaded their customers into trading more and trading faster. Most of those customers ended up picking their own pockets, instead of paying someone else to do it for them—and the cheap commissions on that kind of transaction are a poor consolation for the result. More traditional brokerage firms, meanwhile, began emphasizing financial planning and "integrated asset management," instead of compensating their brokers only on the basis of how many commissions they could generate.

By what must seem a quirk to the outsider there are no formal requirements for being a security analyst. Contrast with this the facts that a customer's broker must pass an examination, meet the required character tests, and be duly accepted and registered by the New York Stock Exchange. As a practical matter, nearly all the younger analysts have had extensive business-school training, and the oldsters have acquired at least the equivalent in the school of long experience. In the great majority of cases, the employing brokerage house can be counted on to assure itself of the qualifications and competence of its analysts.*

The customer of the brokerage firm may deal with the security analysts directly, or his contact may be an indirect one via the customer's broker. In either case the analyst is available to the client for a considerable amount of information and advice. Let us make an emphatic statement here. The value of the security analyst to the investor depends largely on the investor's own attitude. If the investor asks the analyst the right questions, he is likely to get the right—or at least valuable—answers. The analysts hired by brokerage houses, we are convinced, are greatly handicapped by the general feeling that they are supposed to be market analysts as well. When they are asked whether a given common stock is "sound," the question often means, "Is this stock likely to advance during the next few months?" As a result many of them are com-

---

* This remains true, although many of Wall Street's best analysts hold the title of chartered financial analyst. The CFA certification is awarded by the Association of Investment Management & Research (formerly the Financial Analysts Federation) only after the candidate has completed years of rigorous study and passed a series of difficult exams. More than 50,000 analysts worldwide have been certified as CFAs. Sadly, a recent survey by Professor Stanley Block found that most CFAs ignore Graham's teachings: Growth potential ranks higher than quality of earnings, risks, and dividend policy in determining P/E ratios, while far more analysts base their buy ratings on recent price than on the long-term outlook for the company. See Stanley Block, "A Study of Financial Analysts: Practice and Theory," *Financial Analysts Journal*, July/August, 1999, at www.aimrpubs.org. As Graham was fond of saying, his own books have been read by—and ignored by—more people than any other books in finance.

pelled to analyze with one eye on the stock ticker—a pose not conducive to sound thinking or worthwhile conclusions.*

In the next section of this book we shall deal with some of the concepts and possible achievements of security analysis. A great many analysts working for stock exchange firms could be of prime assistance to the bona fide investor who wants to be sure that he gets full value for his money, and possibly a little more. As in the case of the customers' brokers, what is needed at the beginning is a clear understanding by the analyst of the investor's attitude and objectives. Once the analyst is convinced that he is dealing with a man who is value-minded rather than quotation-minded, there is an excellent chance that his recommendations will prove of real overall benefit.

The CFA Certificate for Financial Analysts

An important step was taken in 1963 toward giving professional standing and responsibility to financial analysts. The official title of chartered financial analyst (CFA) is now awarded to those senior practitioners who pass required examinations and meet other tests of fitness.[1] The subjects covered include security analysis and portfolio management. The analogy with the long-established professional title of certified public accountant (CPA) is evident and intentional. This relatively new apparatus of recognition and control should serve to elevate the standards of financial analysts and eventually to place their work on a truly professional basis.†

---

* It is highly unusual today for a security analyst to allow mere commoners to contact him directly. For the most part, only the nobility of institutional investors are permitted to approach the throne of the almighty Wall Street analyst. An individual investor might, perhaps, have some luck calling analysts who work at "regional" brokerage firms headquartered outside of New York City. The investor relations area at the websites of most publicly traded companies will provide a list of analysts who follow the stock. Websites like www.zacks.com and www.multex.com offer access to analysts' research reports—but the intelligent investor should remember that most analysts do not analyze businesses. Instead, they engage in guesswork about future stock prices.

† Benjamin Graham was the prime force behind the establishment of the CFA program, which he advocated for nearly two decades before it became a reality.

Dealings with Brokerage Houses

One of the most disquieting developments of the period in which we write this revision has been the financial embarrassment—in plain words, bankruptcy or near-bankruptcy—of quite a few New York Stock Exchange firms, including at least two of considerable size.* This is the first time in half a century or more that such a thing has happened, and it is startling for more than one reason. For many decades the New York Stock Exchange has been moving in the direction of closer and stricter controls over the operations and financial condition of its members—including minimum capital requirements, surprise audits, and the like. Besides this, we have had 37 years of control over the exchanges and their members by the Securities and Exchange Commission. Finally, the stock-brokerage industry itself has operated under favorable conditions—namely, a huge increase in volume, fixed minimum commission rates (largely eliminating competitive fees), and a limited number of member firms.

The first financial troubles of the brokerage houses (in 1969) were attributed to the increase in volume itself. This, it was claimed, overtaxed their facilities, increased their overhead, and produced many troubles in making financial settlements. It should be pointed out this was probably the first time in history that important enterprises have gone broke because they had more business than they could handle. In 1970, as brokerage failures increased, they were blamed chiefly on "the falling off in volume." A strange complaint when one reflects that the turnover of the

---

* The two firms Graham had in mind were probably Du Pont, Glore, Forgan & Co. and Goodbody & Co. Du Pont (founded by the heirs to the chemical fortune) was saved from insolvency in 1970 only after Texas entrepreneur H. Ross Perot lent more than $50 million to the firm; Goodbody, the fifth-largest brokerage firm in the United States, would have failed in late 1970 had Merrill Lynch not acquired it. Hayden, Stone & Co. would also have gone under if it had not been acquired. In 1970, no fewer than seven brokerage firms went bust. The farcical story of Wall Street's frenzied over-expansion in the late 1960s is beautifully told in John Brooks's *The Go-Go Years* (John Wiley & Sons, New York, 1999).

NYSE in 1970 totaled 2,937 million shares, the *largest* volume in its history and well over twice as large as in any year before 1965. During the 15 years of the bull market ending in 1964 the annual volume had averaged "only" 712 million shares—one quarter of the 1970 figure—but the brokerage business had enjoyed the greatest prosperity in its history. If, as it appears, the member firms as a whole had allowed their overhead and other expenses to increase at a rate that could not sustain even a mild reduction in volume during part of a year, this does not speak well for either their business acumen or their financial conservatism.

A third explanation of the financial trouble finally emerged out of a mist of concealment, and we suspect that it is the most plausible and significant of the three. It seems that a good part of the capital of certain brokerage houses was held in the form of common stocks owned by the individual partners. Some of these seem to have been highly speculative and carried at inflated values. When the market declined in 1969 the quotations of such securities fell drastically and a substantial part of the capital of the firms vanished with them.[2] In effect the partners were speculating with the capital that was supposed to protect the customers against the ordinary financial hazards of the brokerage business, in order to make a double profit thereon. This was inexcusable; we refrain from saying more.

The investor should use his intelligence not only in formulating his financial policies but also in the associated details. These include the choice of a reputable broker to execute his orders. Up to now it was sufficient to counsel our readers to deal only with a member of the New York Stock Exchange, unless he had compelling reasons to use a nonmember firm. Reluctantly, we must add some further advice in this area. We think that people who do not carry margin accounts—and in our vocabulary this means *all* nonprofessional *investors*—should have the delivery and receipt of their securities handled by their bank. When giving a buying order to your brokers you can instruct them to deliver the securities bought to your bank against payment therefor by the bank; conversely, when selling you can instruct your bank to deliver the securities to the broker against payment of the proceeds. These services will cost a little extra but they should be well worth the expense in terms of safety and peace of mind. This advice may be disregarded, as no longer called for, after the investor is sure that all the problems of stock-exchange firms have been disposed of, but not before.*

Investment Bankers

The term "investment banker" is applied to a firm that engages to an important extent in originating, underwriting, and selling new issues of stocks and bonds. (To underwrite means to guarantee to the issuing corporation, or other issuer, that the security will be fully sold.) A number of the brokerage houses carry on a certain amount of underwriting activity. Generally this is confined to participating in underwriting groups formed by leading investment bankers. There is an additional tendency for brokerage firms to originate and sponsor a minor amount of new-issue financing, particularly in the form of smaller issues of common stocks when a bull market is in full swing.

Investment banking is perhaps the most respectable department of the Wall Street community, because it is here that finance plays its constructive role of supplying new capital for the expansion of industry. In fact, much of the theoretical justification for maintaining active stock markets, notwithstanding their frequent speculative excesses, lies in the fact that organized security exchanges facilitate the sale of new issues of bonds and stocks. If investors or speculators could not expect to see a ready market for a new security offered them, they might well refuse to buy it.

The relationship between the investment banker and the

---

* Nearly all brokerage transactions are now conducted electronically, and securities are no longer physically "delivered." Thanks to the establishment of the Securities Investor Protection Corporation, or SIPC, in 1970, investors are generally assured of recovering their full account values if their brokerage firm becomes insolvent. SIPC is a government-mandated consortium of brokers; all the members agree to pool their assets to cover losses incurred by the customers of any firm that becomes insolvent. SIPC's protection eliminates the need for investors to make payment and take delivery through a bank intermediary, as Graham urges.

investor is basically that of the salesman to the prospective buyer. For many years past the great bulk of the new offerings in dollar value has consisted of bond issues that were purchased in the main by financial institutions such as banks and insurance companies. In this business the security salesmen have been dealing with shrewd and experienced buyers. Hence any recommendations made by the investment bankers to these customers have had to pass careful and skeptical scrutiny. Thus these transactions are almost always effected on a businesslike footing.

But a different situation obtains in a relationship between the *individual* security buyer and the investment banking firms, including the stockbrokers acting as underwriters. Here the purchaser is frequently inexperienced and seldom shrewd. He is easily influenced by what the salesman tells him, especially in the case of common-stock issues, since often his unconfessed desire in buying is chiefly to make a quick profit. The effect of all this is that the public investor's protection lies less in his own critical faculty than in the scruples and ethics of the offering houses.[3]

It is a tribute to the honesty and competence of the underwriting firms that they are able to combine fairly well the discordant roles of adviser and salesman. But it is imprudent for the buyer to trust himself to the judgment of the seller. In 1959 we stated at this point: "The bad results of this unsound attitude show themselves recurrently in the underwriting field and with notable effects in the sale of new common stock issues during periods of active speculation." Shortly thereafter this warning proved urgently needed. As already pointed out, the years 1960–61 and, again, 1968–69 were marked by an unprecedented outpouring of issues of lowest quality, sold to the public at absurdly high offering prices and in many cases pushed much higher by heedless speculation and some semi-manipulation. A number of the more important Wall Street houses have participated to some degree in these less than creditable activities, which demonstrates that the familiar combination of greed, folly, and irresponsibility has not been exorcized from the financial scene.

The intelligent investor will pay attention to the advice and recommendations received from investment banking houses, especially those known by him to have an excellent reputation; but he will be sure to bring sound and independent judgment to bear upon these suggestions—either his own, if he is competent, or that of some other type of adviser.*

Other Advisers

It is a good old custom, especially in the smaller towns, to consult one's local banker about investments. A commercial banker may not be a thoroughgoing expert on security values, but he is experienced and conservative. He is especially useful to the unskilled investor, who is often tempted to stray from the straight and unexciting path of a defensive policy and needs the steadying influence of a prudent mind. The more alert and aggressive investor, seeking counsel in the selection of security bargains, will not ordinarily find the commercial banker's viewpoint to be especially suited to his own objectives.†

We take a more critical attitude toward the widespread custom of asking investment advice from relatives or friends. The inquirer always thinks he has good reason for assuming that the person consulted has superior knowledge or experience. Our own observation indicates that it is almost as difficult to select satisfactory lay advisers as it is to select the proper securities unaided. Much bad advice is given free.

Summary

Investors who are prepared to pay a fee for the management of their funds may wisely select some well-established and well-recommended investment-counsel firm. Alternatively, they may use the investment department of a large trust company or the supervisory service supplied on a fee basis by a few of the leading New York Stock Exchange houses. The results to be expected are in no wise exceptional, but they are commensurate with those of the average well-informed and cautious investor.

---

* Those who heeded Graham's advice would not have been suckered into buying Internet IPOs in 1999 and 2000.

† This traditional role of bankers has for the most part been supplanted by accountants, lawyers, or financial planners.

Most security buyers obtain advice without paying for it specifically. It stands to reason, therefore, that in the majority of cases they are not entitled to and should not expect better than average results. They should be wary of all persons, whether customers' brokers or security salesmen, who promise spectacular income or profits. This applies both to the selection of securities and to guidance in the elusive (and perhaps illusive) art of trading in the market.

Defensive investors, as we have defined them, will not ordinarily be equipped to pass independent judgment on the security recommendations made by their advisers. But they can be explicit—and even repetitiously so—in stating the kind of securities they want to buy. If they follow our prescription they will confine themselves to high-grade bonds and the common stocks of leading corporations, preferably those that can be purchased at individual price levels that are not high in the light of experience and analysis. The security analyst of any reputable stock-exchange house can make up a suitable list of such common stocks and can certify to the investor whether or not the existing price level therefor is a reasonably conservative one as judged by past experience.

The aggressive investor will ordinarily work in active cooperation with his advisers. He will want their recommendations explained in detail, and he will insist on passing his own judgment upon them. This means that the investor will gear his expectations and the character of his security operations to the development of his own knowledge and experience in the field. Only in the exceptional case, where the integrity and competence of the advisers have been thoroughly demonstrated, should the investor act upon the advice of others without understanding and approving the decision made.

There have always been unprincipled stock salesmen and fly-by-night stock brokers, and—as a matter of course—we have advised our readers to confine their dealings, if possible, to members of the New York Stock Exchange. But we are reluctantly compelled to add the extra-cautious counsel that security deliveries and payments be made through the intermediary of the investor's bank. The distressing Wall Street brokerage-house picture may have cleared up completely in a few years, but in late 1971 we still suggest, "Better safe than sorry."

COMMENTARY ON CHAPTER 10

I feel grateful to the Milesian wench who, seeing the philoso-
pher Thales continually spending his time in contemplation of
the heavenly vault and always keeping his eyes raised upward,
put something in his way to make him stumble, to warn him
that it would be time to amuse his thoughts with things in the
clouds when he had seen to those at his feet. Indeed she
gave him or her good counsel, to look rather to himself than
to the sky.

—Michel de Montaigne

DO YOU NEED HELP?

In the glory days of the late 1990s, many investors chose to go it alone.
By doing their own research, picking stocks themselves, and placing
their trades through an online broker, these investors bypassed Wall
Street's costly infrastructure of research, advice, and trading. Unfortunately, many do-it-yourselfers asserted their independence right before
the worst bear market since the Great Depression—making them feel,
in the end, that they were fools for going it alone. That's not necessarily true, of course; people who delegated every decision to a traditional
stockbroker lost money, too.

But many investors do take comfort from the experience, judgment,
and second opinion that a good financial adviser can provide. Some
investors may need an outsider to show them what rate of return they
need to earn on their investments, or how much extra money they
need to save, in order to meet their financial goals. Others may simply
benefit from having someone else to blame when their investments go
down; that way, instead of beating yourself up in an agony of self-
doubt, you get to criticize someone who typically can defend him or
herself and encourage you at the same time. That may provide just the
psychological boost you need to keep investing steadily at a time

when other investors' hearts may fail them. All in all, just as there's no reason you can't manage your own portfolio, so there's no shame in seeking professional help in managing it.[1]

How can you tell if you need a hand? Here are some signals:

Big losses. If your portfolio lost more than 40% of its value from the beginning of 2000 through the end of 2002, then you did even worse than the dismal performance of the stock market itself. It hardly matters whether you blew it by being lazy, reckless, or just unlucky; after such a giant loss, your portfolio is crying out for help.

Busted budgets. If you perennially struggle to make ends meet, have no idea where your money goes, find it impossible to save on a regular schedule, and chronically fail to pay your bills on time, then your finances are out of control. An adviser can help you get a grip on your money by designing a comprehensive financial plan that will outline how—and how much—you should spend, borrow, save, and invest.

Chaotic portfolios. All too many investors thought they were diversified in the late 1990s because they owned 39 "different" Internet stocks, or seven "different" U.S. growth-stock funds. But that's like thinking that an all-soprano chorus can handle singing "Old Man River" better than a soprano soloist can. No matter how many sopranos you add, that chorus will never be able to nail all those low notes until some baritones join the group. Likewise, if all your holdings go up and down together, you lack the investing harmony that true diversification brings. A professional "asset-allocation" plan can help.

Major changes. If you've become self-employed and need to set up a retirement plan, your aging parents don't have their finances in order, or college for your kids looks unaffordable, an adviser can not only provide peace of mind but help you make genuine improvements in the quality of your life. What's more, a qualified professional can ensure that you benefit from and comply with the staggering complexity of the tax laws and retirement rules.

TRUST, THEN VERIFY

Remember that financial con artists thrive by talking you into trusting them and by talking you out of investigating them. Before you place

---

[1] For a particularly thoughtful discussion of these issues, see Walter Updegrave, "Advice on Advice," *Money,* January, 2003, pp. 53–55.

your financial future in the hands of an adviser, it's imperative that you find someone who not only makes you comfortable but whose honesty is beyond reproach. As Ronald Reagan used to say, "Trust, then verify." Start off by thinking of the handful of people you know best and trust the most. Then ask if they can refer you to an adviser whom *they* trust and who, they feel, delivers good value for his fees. A vote of confidence from someone you admire is a good start.[2]

Once you have the name of the adviser and his firm, as well as his specialty—is he a stockbroker? financial planner? accountant? insurance agent?—you can begin your due diligence. Enter the name of the adviser and his or her firm into an Internet search engine like Google to see if anything comes up (watch for terms like "fine," "complaint," "lawsuit," "disciplinary action," or "suspension"). If the adviser is a stockbroker or insurance agent, contact the office of your state's securities commissioner (a convenient directory of online links is at www.nasaa.org) to ask whether any disciplinary actions or customer complaints have been filed against the adviser.[3] If you're considering an accountant who also functions as a financial adviser, your state's accounting regulators (whom you can find through the National Association of State Boards of Accountancy at www.nasba.org) will tell you whether his or her record is clean.

Financial planners (or their firms) must register with either the U.S. Securities and Exchange Commission or securities regulators in the state where their practice is based. As part of that registration, the adviser must file a two-part document called Form ADV. You should be able to view and download it at www.advisorinfo.sec.gov, www.iard. com, or the website of your state securities regulator. Pay special attention to the Disclosure Reporting Pages, where the adviser must disclose any disciplinary actions by regulators. (Because unscrupu-

---

[2] If you're unable to get a referral from someone you trust, you may be able to find a fee-only financial planner through www.napfa.org (or www.feeonly. org), whose members are generally held to high standards of service and integrity.

[3] By itself, a customer complaint is not enough to disqualify an adviser from your consideration; but a persistent pattern of complaints is. And a disciplinary action by state or Federal regulators usually tells you to find another adviser. Another source for checking a broker's record is http://pdpi.nasdr. com/PDPI.

lous advisers have been known to remove those pages before handing an ADV to a prospective client, you should independently obtain your own complete copy.) It's a good idea to cross-check a financial planner's record at www.cfp-board.org, since some planners who have been disciplined outside their home state can fall through the regulatory cracks. For more tips on due diligence, see the sidebar below.

WORDS OF WARNING

The need for due diligence doesn't stop once you hire an adviser. Melanie Senter Lubin, securities commissioner for the State of Maryland, suggests being on guard for words and phrases that can spell trouble. If your adviser keeps saying them—or twisting your arm to do anything that makes you uncomfortable—"then get in touch with the authorities very quickly," warns Lubin. Here's the kind of lingo that should set off warning bells:

"offshore"

"the opportunity of a
   lifetime"

"prime bank"

"This baby's gonna
   move."

"guaranteed"

"You need to hurry."

"It's a sure thing."

"our proprietary
   computer model"

"The smart money is
   buying it."

"options strategy"

"It's a no-brainer."

"You can't afford not to
   own it."

"We can beat the
   market."

"You'll be sorry if you
   don't . . ."

"exclusive"

"You should focus on
   performance, not
   fees."

"Don't you want to be
   rich?"

"can't lose"

"The upside is huge."

"There's no downside."

"I'm putting my mother
   in it."

"Trust me."

"commodities trading"

"monthly returns"

"active asset-allocation
   strategy"

"We can cap your
   downside."

"No one else knows how
   to do this."

GETTING TO KNOW YOU

A leading financial-planning newsletter recently canvassed dozens of advisers to get their thoughts on how you should go about interviewing them.[4] In screening an adviser, your goals should be to:

- determine whether he or she cares about helping clients, or just goes through the motions
- establish whether he or she understands the fundamental principles of investing as they are outlined in this book
- assess whether he or she is sufficiently educated, trained, and experienced to help you.

Here are some of the questions that prominent financial planners recommended any prospective client should ask:

Why are you in this business? What is the mission statement of your firm? Besides your alarm clock, what makes you get up in the morning?

What is your investing philosophy? Do you use stocks or mutual funds? Do you use technical analysis? Do you use market timing? (A "yes" to either of the last two questions is a "no" signal to you.)

Do you focus solely on asset management, or do you also advise on taxes, estate and retirement planning, budgeting and debt management, and insurance? How do your education, experience, and credentials qualify you to give those kinds of financial advice?[5]

What needs do your clients typically have in common? How can you help me achieve my goals? How will you track and report my progress? Do you provide a checklist that I can use to monitor the implementation of any financial plan we develop?

---

[4] Robert Veres, editor and publisher of the *Inside Information* newsletter, generously shared these responses for this book. Other checklists of questions can be found at www.cfp-board.org and www.napfa.org.

[5] Credentials like the CFA, CFP, or CPA tell you that the adviser has taken and passed a rigorous course of study. (Most of the other "alphabet soup" of credentials brandished by financial planners, including the "CFM" or the "CMFC," signify very little.) More important, by contacting the organization that awards the credential, you can verify his record and check that he has not been disciplined for violations of rules or ethics.

How do you choose investments? What investing approach do you believe is most successful, and what evidence can you show me that you have achieved that kind of success for your clients? What do you do when an investment performs poorly for an entire year? (Any adviser who answers "sell" is not worth hiring.)

Do you, when recommending investments, accept any form of compensation from any third party? Why or why not? Under which circumstances? How much, in actual dollars, do you estimate I would pay for your services the first year? What would make that number go up or down over time? (If fees will consume more than 1% of your assets annually, you should probably shop for another adviser.[6])

How many clients do you have, and how often do you communicate with them? What has been your proudest achievement for a client? What characteristics do your favorite clients share? What's the worst experience you've had with a client, and how did you resolve it? What determines whether a client speaks to you or to your support staff? How long do clients typically stay with you?

Can I see a sample account statement? (If you can't understand it, ask the adviser to explain it. If you can't understand his explanation, he's not right for you.)

Do you consider yourself financially successful? Why? How do you define financial success?

How high an average annual return do you think is feasible on my investments? (Anything over 8% to10% is unrealistic.)

Will you provide me with your résumé, your Form ADV, and at least three references? (If the adviser or his firm is required to file an ADV, and he will not provide you a copy, get up and leave—and keep one hand on your wallet as you go.)

Have you ever had a formal complaint filed against you? Why did the last client who fired you do so?

---

[6] If you have less than $100,000 to invest, you may not be able to find a financial adviser who will take your account. In that case, buy a diversified basket of low-cost index funds, follow the behavioral advice throughout this book, and your portfolio should eventually grow to the level at which you can afford an adviser.

DEFEATING YOUR OWN WORST ENEMY

Finally, bear in mind that great financial advisers do not grow on trees. Often, the best already have as many clients as they can handle—and may be willing to take you on only if you seem like a good match. So they will ask you some tough questions as well, which might include:

Why do you feel you need a financial adviser?

What are your long-term goals?

What has been your greatest frustration in dealing with other advisers (including yourself)?

Do you have a budget? Do you live within your means? What percentage of your assets do you spend each year?

When we look back a year from now, what will I need to have accomplished in order for you to be happy with your progress?

How do you handle conflicts or disagreements?

How did you respond emotionally to the bear market that began in 2000?

What are your worst financial fears? Your greatest financial hopes?

What rate of return on your investments do you consider reasonable? (Base your answer on Chapter 3.)

An adviser who doesn't ask questions like these—and who does not show enough interest in you to sense intuitively what other questions you consider to be the right ones—is not a good fit.

Above all else, you should trust your adviser enough to permit him or her to protect you from your worst enemy—yourself. "You hire an adviser," explains commentator Nick Murray, "not to manage money but to manage you."

"If the adviser is a line of defense between you and your worst impulsive tendencies," says financial-planning analyst Robert Veres, "then he or she should have systems in place that will help the two of you control them." Among those systems:

- a **comprehensive financial plan** that outlines how you will earn, save, spend, borrow, and invest your money;
- an **investment policy statement** that spells out your fundamental approach to investing;
- an **asset-allocation plan** that details how much money you will keep in different investment categories.

These are the building blocks on which good financial decisions must be founded, and they should be created mutually—by you and the adviser—rather than imposed unilaterally. You should not invest a dollar or make a decision until you are satisfied that these foundations are in place and in accordance with your wishes.

CHAPTER 11

Security Analysis for the Lay Investor: General Approach

*F*inancial analysis is now a well-established and flourishing profession, or semiprofession. The various societies of analysts that make up the National Federation of Financial Analysts have over 13,000 members, most of whom make their living out of this branch of mental activity. Financial analysts have textbooks, a code of ethics, and a quarterly journal.* They also have their share of unresolved problems. In recent years there has been a tendency to replace the general concept of "security analysis" by that of "financial analysis." The latter phrase has a broader implication and is better suited to describe the work of most senior analysts on Wall Street. It would be useful to think of security analysis as limiting itself pretty much to the examination and evaluation of stocks and bonds, whereas financial analysis would comprise that work, plus the determination of investment policy (portfolio selection), plus a substantial amount of general economic analysis.[1] In this chapter we shall use whatever designation is most applicable, with chief emphasis on the work of the security analyst proper.

The security analyst deals with the past, the present, and the future of any given security issue. He describes the business; he summarizes its operating results and financial position; he sets forth its strong and weak points, its possibilities and risks; he estimates its future earning power under various assumptions, or as a

---

* The National Federation of Financial Analysts is now the Association for Investment Management and Research; its "quarterly" research publication, the *Financial Analysts Journal,* now appears every other month.

"best guess." He makes elaborate comparisons of various companies, or of the same company at various times. Finally, he expresses an opinion as to the safety of the issue, if it is a bond or investment-grade preferred stock, or as to its attractiveness as a purchase, if it is a common stock.

In doing all these things the security analyst avails himself of a number of techniques, ranging from the elementary to the most abstruse. He may modify substantially the figures in the company's annual statements, even though they bear the sacred *imprimatur* of the certified public accountant. He is on the lookout particularly for items in these reports that may mean a good deal more or less than they say.

The security analyst develops and applies standards of safety by which we can conclude whether a given bond or preferred stock may be termed sound enough to justify purchase for investment. These standards relate primarily to past average earnings, but they are concerned also with capital structure, working capital, asset values, and other matters.

In dealing with common stocks the security analyst until recently has only rarely applied standards of value as well defined as were his standards of safety for bonds and preferred stocks. Most of the time he contended himself with a summary of past performances, a more or less general forecast of the future—with particular emphasis on the next 12 months—and a rather arbitrary conclusion. The latter was, and still is, often drawn with one eye on the stock ticker or the market charts. In the past few years, however, much attention has been given by practicing analysts to the problem of valuing growth stocks. Many of these have sold at such high prices in relation to past and current earnings that those recommending them have felt a special obligation to justify their purchase by fairly definite projections of expected earnings running fairly far into the future. Certain mathematical techniques of a rather sophisticated sort have perforce been invoked to support the valuations arrived at.

We shall deal with these techniques, in foreshortened form, a little later. However, we must point out a troublesome paradox here, which is that the mathematical valuations have become most prevalent precisely in those areas where one might consider them least reliable. For the more dependent the valuation becomes on anticipations of the future—and the less it is tied to a figure demonstrated by past performance—the more vulnerable it becomes to possible miscalculation and serious error. A large part of the value found for a high-multiplier growth stock is derived from future projections which differ markedly from past performance—except perhaps in the growth rate itself. Thus it may be said that security analysts today find themselves compelled to become most mathematical and "scientific" in the very situations which lend themselves least auspiciously to exact treatment.*

Let us proceed, nonetheless, with our discussion of the more important elements and techniques of security analysis. The present highly condensed treatment is directed to the needs of the nonprofessional investor. At the minimum he should understand what the security analyst is talking about and driving at; beyond that, he should be equipped, if possible, to distinguish between superficial and sound analysis.

Security analysis for the lay investor is thought of as beginning

---

* The higher the growth rate you project, and the longer the future period over which you project it, the more sensitive your forecast becomes to the slightest error. If, for instance, you estimate that a company earning $1 per share can raise that profit by 15% a year for the next 15 years, its earnings would end up at $8.14. If the market values the company at 35 times earnings, the stock would finish the period at roughly $285. But if earnings grow at 14% instead of 15%, the company would earn $7.14 at the end of the period—and, in the shock of that shortfall, investors would no longer be willing to pay 35 times earnings. At, say, 20 times earnings, the stock would end up around $140 per share, or more than 50% less. Because advanced mathematics gives the appearance of precision to the inherently iffy process of foreseeing the future, investors must be highly skeptical of anyone who claims to hold any complex computational key to basic financial problems. As Graham put it: "In 44 years of Wall Street experience and study, I have never seen dependable calculations made about common-stock values, or related investment policies, that went beyond simple arithmetic or the most elementary algebra. Whenever calculus is brought in, or higher algebra, you could take it as a warning signal that the operator was trying to substitute theory for experience, and usually also to give to speculation the deceptive guise of investment." (See p. 570.)

with the interpretation of a company's annual financial report. This is a subject which we have covered for laymen in a separate book, entitled *The Interpretation of Financial Statements*.[2] We do not consider it necessary or appropriate to traverse the same ground in this chapter, especially since the emphasis in the present book is on principles and attitudes rather than on information and description. Let us pass on to two basic questions underlying the selection of investments. What are the primary tests of safety of a corporate bond or preferred stock? What are the chief factors entering into the valuation of a common stock?

Bond Analysis

The most dependable and hence the most respectable branch of security analysis concerns itself with the safety, or quality, of bond issues and investment-grade preferred stocks. The chief criterion used for corporate bonds is the number of times that total interest charges have been covered by available earnings for some years in the past. In the case of preferred stocks, it is the number of times that bond interest and preferred dividends combined have been covered.

The exact standards applied will vary with different authorities. Since the tests are at bottom arbitrary, there is no way to determine precisely the most suitable criteria. In the 1961 revision of our textbook, *Security Analysis*, we recommend certain "coverage" standards, which appear in Table 11-1.*

Our basic test is applied only to the *average* results for a period of years. Other authorities require also that a *minimum* coverage be shown for every year considered. We approve a "poorest-year" test

---

* In 1972, an investor in corporate bonds had little choice but to assemble his or her own portfolio. Today, roughly 500 mutual funds invest in corporate bonds, creating a convenient, well-diversified bundle of securities. Since it is not feasible to build a diversified bond portfolio on your own unless you have at least $100,000, the typical intelligent investor will be best off simply buying a low-cost bond fund and leaving the painstaking labor of credit research to its managers. For more on bond funds, see the commentary on Chapter 4.

TABLE 11-1   Recommended Minimum "Coverage" for Bonds and Preferred Stocks

A. For Investment-grade Bonds

Minimum Ratio of Earnings to Total Fixed Charges:

| | *Before Income Taxes* | | *After Income Taxes* | |
Type of enterprise	Average of Past 7 Years	Alternative: Measured by "Poorest Year"	Average of Past 7 Years	Alternative: Measured by "Poorest Year"
Public-utility operating company	4 times	3 times	2.65 times	2.10 times
Railroad	5	4	3.20	2.65
Industrial	7	5	4.30	3.20
Retail concern	5	4	3.20	2.65

B. For Investment-grade Preferred Stocks

The same minimum figures as above are required to be shown by the ratio of earnings *before* income taxes to the sum of fixed charges plus twice preferred dividends.

NOTE: The inclusion of twice the preferred dividends allows for the fact that preferred dividends are not income-tax deductible, whereas interest charges are so deductible.

C. Other Categories of Bonds and Preferreds

The standards given above are not applicable to (1) public-utility holding companies, (2) financial companies, (3) real-estate companies. Requirements for these special groups are omitted here.

as an *alternative* to the seven-year-average test; it would be sufficient if the bond or preferred stock met either of these criteria.

It may be objected that the large increase in bond interest rates since 1961 would justify some offsetting reduction in the coverage of charges required. Obviously it would be much harder for an industrial company to show a seven-times coverage of interest charges at 8% than at 4½%. To meet this changed situation we now suggest an alternative requirement related to the percent earned on the *principal* amount of the debt. These figures might be 33% before taxes for an industrial company, 20% for a public utility, and 25% for a railroad. It should be borne in mind here that the rate actually paid by most companies on their total debt is considerably less than the current 8% figures, since they have the benefit of older issues bearing lower coupons. The "poorest year" requirement could be set at about two-thirds of the seven-year requirement.

In addition to the earnings-coverage test, a number of others are generally applied. These include the following:

1. *Size of Enterprise.* There is a minimum standard in terms of volume of business for a corporation—varying as between industrials, utilities, and railroads—and of population for a municipality.

2. *Stock/Equity Ratio.* This is the ratio of the market price of the junior stock issues* to the total face amount of the debt, or the debt plus preferred stock. It is a rough measure of the protection, or "cushion," afforded by the presence of a junior investment that must first bear the brunt of unfavorable developments. This factor includes the market's appraisal of the future prospects of the enterprise.

3. *Property Value.* The asset values, as shown on the balance sheet or as appraised, were formerly considered the chief security and protection for a bond issue. Experience has shown that in most cases safety resides in the earning power, and if this is deficient the assets lose most of their reputed value. Asset values, however, retain importance as a separate test of ample security for bonds and preferred stocks in three enterprise groups: public utilities (because rates may depend largely on the property investment), real-estate concerns, and investment companies.

At this point the alert investor should ask, "How dependable are tests of safety that are measured by past and present performance, in view of the fact that payment of interest and principal depends upon what the future will bring forth?" The answer can be founded

---

* By "junior stock issues" Graham means shares of common stock. Preferred stock is considered "senior" to common stock because the company must pay all dividends on the preferred before paying any dividends on the common.

only on experience. Investment history shows that bonds and preferred stocks that have met stringent tests of safety, based on the
past, have in the great majority of cases been able to face the vicissitudes of the future successfully. This has been strikingly demonstrated in the major field of railroad bonds—a field that has been
marked by a calamitous frequency of bankruptcies and serious
losses. In nearly every case the roads that got into trouble had long
been overbonded, had shown an inadequate coverage of fixed
charges in periods of average prosperity, and would thus have been
ruled out by investors who applied strict tests of safety. Conversely,
practically every road that has met such tests has escaped financial
embarrassment. Our premise was strikingly vindicated by the
financial history of the numerous railroads reorganized in the 1940s
and in 1950. All of these, with one exception, started their careers
with fixed charges reduced to a point where the current coverage of
fixed-interest requirements was ample, or at least respectable. The
exception was the New Haven Railroad, which in its reorganization
year, 1947, earned its new charges only about 1.1 times. In conse-
quence, while all the other roads were able to come through rather
difficult times with solvency unimpaired, the New Haven relapsed
into trusteeship (for the third time) in 1961.

In Chapter 17 below we shall consider some aspects of the bankruptcy of the Penn Central Railroad, which shook the financial
community in 1970. An elementary fact in this case was that the
coverage of fixed charges did not meet conservative standards as
early as 1965; hence a prudent bond investor would have avoided
or disposed of the bond issues of the system long before its financial collapse.

Our observations on the adequacy of the past record to judge
future safety apply, and to an even greater degree, to the public
utilities, which constitute a major area for bond investment.
Receivership of a soundly capitalized (electric) utility company or
system is almost impossible. Since Securities and Exchange Commission control was instituted,* along with the breakup of most of

---

* After investors lost billions of dollars on the shares of recklessly assem-
bled utility companies in 1929–1932, Congress authorized the SEC to reg-
ulate the issuance of utility stocks under the Public Utility Holding Company
Act of 1935.

the holding-company systems, public-utility financing has been sound and bankruptcies unknown. The financial troubles of electric and gas utilities in the 1930s were traceable almost 100% to financial excesses and mismanagement, which left their imprint clearly on the companies' capitalization structures. Simple but stringent tests of safety, therefore, would have warned the investor away from the issues that were later to default.

Among industrial bond issues the long-term record has been different. Although the industrial group as a whole has shown a better growth of earning power than either the railroads or the utilities, it has revealed a lesser degree of inherent stability for individual companies and lines of business. Thus in the past, at least, there have been persuasive reasons for confining the purchase of industrial bonds and preferred stocks to companies that not only are of major size but also have shown an ability in the past to withstand a serious depression.

Few defaults of industrial bonds have occurred since 1950, but this fact is attributable in part to the absence of a major depression during this long period. Since 1966 there have been adverse developments in the financial position of many industrial companies. Considerable difficulties have developed as the result of unwise expansion. On the one hand this has involved large additions to both bank loans and long-term debt; on the other it has frequently produced operating losses instead of the expected profits. At the beginning of 1971 it was calculated that in the past seven years the interest payments of all nonfinancial firms had grown from $9.8 billion in 1963 to $26.1 billion in 1970, and that interest payments had taken 29% of the aggregate profits before interest and taxes in 1971, against only 16% in 1963.[3] Obviously, the burden on many individual firms had increased much more than this. Overbonded companies have become all too familiar. There is every reason to repeat the caution expressed in our 1965 edition:

> We are not quite ready to suggest that the investor may count on an indefinite continuance of this favorable situation, and hence relax his standards of bond selection in the industrial or any other group.

Common-Stock Analysis

The ideal form of common-stock analysis leads to a valuation of the issue which can be compared with the current price to determine whether or not the security is an attractive purchase. This valuation, in turn, would ordinarily be found by estimating the average earnings over a period of years in the *future* and then multiplying that estimate by an appropriate "capitalization factor."

The now-standard procedure for estimating future earning power starts with average *past* data for physical volume, prices received, and operating margin. Future sales in dollars are then projected on the basis of assumptions as to the amount of change in volume and price level over the previous base. These estimates, in turn, are grounded first on general economic forecasts of gross national product, and then on special calculations applicable to the industry and company in question.

An illustration of this method of valuation may be taken from our 1965 edition and brought up to date by adding the sequel. The Value Line, a leading investment service, makes forecasts of future earnings and dividends by the procedure outlined above, and then derives a figure of "price potentiality" (or projected market value) by applying a valuation formula to each issue based largely on certain past relationships. In Table 11-2 we reproduce the projections for 1967–1969 made in June 1964, and compare them with the earnings, and average market price actually realized in 1968 (which approximates the 1967–1969 period).

The combined forecasts proved to be somewhat on the low side, but not seriously so. The corresponding predictions made six years before had turned out to be overoptimistic on earnings and dividends; but this had been offset by use of a low multiplier, with the result that the "price potentiality" figure proved to be about the same as the actual average price for 1963.

The reader will note that quite a number of the individual forecasts were wide of the mark. This is an instance in support of our general view that composite or group estimates are likely to be a good deal more dependable than those for individual companies. Ideally, perhaps, the security analyst should pick out the three or four companies whose future he thinks he knows the best, and concentrate his own and his clients' interest on what he forecasts for

TABLE 11-2　The Dow Jones Industrial Average

(The Value Line's Forecast for 1967–1969 (Made in Mid-1964) Compared With Actual Results in 1968)

	Earnings		Price	Price	Average
	Forecast 1967–1969	Actual 1968[a]	June 30 1964	Forecast 1967–1969	Price 1968[a]
Allied Chemical	$3.70	$1.46	54½	67	36½
Aluminum Corp. of Am.	3.85	4.75	71½	85	79
American Can	3.50	4.25	47	57	48
American Tel. & Tel.	4.00	3.75	73½	68	53
American Tobacco	3.00	4.38	51½	33	37
Anaconda	6.00	8.12	44½	70	106
Bethlehem Steel	3.25	3.55	36½	45	31
Chrysler	4.75	6.23	48½	45	60
Du Pont	8.50	7.82	253	240	163
Eastman Kodak	5.00	9.32	133	100	320
General Electric	4.50	3.95	80	90	90½
General Foods	4.70	4.16	88	71	84½
General Motors	6.25	6.02	88	78	81½
Goodyear Tire	3.25	4.12	43	43	54
Internat. Harvester	5.75	5.38	82	63	69
Internat. Nickel	5.20	3.86	79	83	76
Internat. Paper	2.25	2.04	32	36	33
Johns Manville	4.00	4.78	57½	54	71½
Owens-Ill. Glass	5.25	6.20	99	100	125½
Procter & Gamble	4.20	4.30	83	70	91
Sears Roebuck	4.70	5.46	118	78	122½
Standard Oil of Cal.	5.25	5.59	64½	60	67
Standard Oil of N.J.	6.00	5.94	87	73	76
Swift & Co.	3.85	3.41[b]	54	50	57
Texaco	5.50	6.04	79½	70	81
Union Carbide	7.35	5.20	126½	165	90
United Aircraft	4.00	7.65	49½	50	106
U.S. Steel	4.50	4.69	57½	60	42
Westinghouse Elec.	3.25	3.49	30½	50	69
Woolworth	2.25	2.29	29½	32	29½
Total	138.25	149.20	2222	2186	2450
DJIA (Total % 2.67)	52.00	56.00	832	820	918[c]
DJIA Actual 1968	57.89				906[c]
DJIA Actual 1967–1969	56.26				

[a] Adjusted for stock-splits since 1964.
[b] Average 1967–1969.
[c] Difference due to changed divisor.

them. Unfortunately, it appears to be almost impossible to distinguish in advance between those individual forecasts which can be relied upon and those which are subject to a large chance of error. At bottom, this is the reason for the wide diversification practiced by the investment funds. For it is undoubtedly better to concentrate on one stock that you *know* is going to prove highly profitable, rather than dilute your results to a mediocre figure, merely for diversification's sake. But this is not done, because it cannot be done *dependably*.[4] The prevalence of wide diversification is in itself a pragmatic repudiation of the fetish of "selectivity," to which Wall Street constantly pays lip service.*

Factors Affecting the Capitalization Rate

Though average future earnings are supposed to be the chief determinant of value, the security analyst takes into account a number of other factors of a more or less definite nature. Most of these will enter into his capitalization rate, which can vary over a wide range, depending upon the "quality" of the stock issue. Thus, although two companies may have the same figure of expected

---

* In more recent years, most mutual funds have almost robotically mimicked the Standard & Poor's 500-stock index, lest any different holdings cause their returns to deviate from that of the index. In a countertrend, some fund companies have launched what they call "focused" portfolios, which own 25 to 50 stocks that the managers declare to be their "best ideas." That leaves investors wondering whether the other funds run by the same managers contain their worst ideas. Considering that most of the "best idea" funds do not markedly outperform the averages, investors are also entitled to wonder whether the managers' ideas are even worth having in the first place. For indisputably skilled investors like Warren Buffett, wide diversification would be foolish, since it would water down the concentrated force of a few great ideas. But for the typical fund manager or individual investor, *not* diversifying is foolish, since it is so difficult to select a limited number of stocks that will include most winners and exclude most losers. As you own more stocks, the damage any single loser can cause will decline, and the odds of owning all the big winners will rise. The ideal choice for most investors is a total stock market index fund, a low-cost way to hold every stock worth owning.

earnings per share in 1973–1975—say $4—the analyst may value one as low as 40 and the other as high as 100. Let us deal briefly with some of the considerations that enter into these divergent multipliers.

1. *General Long-Term Prospects.* No one really knows anything about what will happen in the distant future, but analysts and investors have strong views on the subject just the same. These views are reflected in the substantial differentials between the price/earnings ratios of individual companies and of industry groups. At this point we added in our 1965 edition:

> For example, at the end of 1963 the chemical companies in the DJIA were selling at considerably higher multipliers than the oil companies, indicating stronger confidence in the prospects of the former than of the latter. Such distinctions made by the market are often soundly based, but when dictated mainly by past performance they are as likely to be wrong as right.

We shall supply here, in Table 11-3, the 1963 year-end material on the chemical and oil company issues in the DJIA, and carry their earnings to the end of 1970. It will be seen that the chemical companies, despite their high multipliers, made practically no gain in earnings in the period after 1963. The oil companies did much better than the chemicals and about in line with the growth implied in their 1963 multipliers.[5] Thus our chemical-stock example proved to be one of the cases in which the market multipliers were proven wrong.*

---

* Graham's point about chemical and oil companies in the 1960s applies to nearly every industry in nearly every time period. Wall Street's consensus view of the future for any given sector is usually either too optimistic or too pessimistic. Worse, the consensus is at its most cheery just when the stocks are most overpriced—and gloomiest just when they are cheapest. The most recent example, of course, is technology and telecommunications stocks, which hit record highs when their future seemed brightest in 1999 and early 2000, and then crashed all the way through 2002. History proves that Wall Street's "expert" forecasters are equally inept at predicting the

TABLE 11-3   Performance of Chemical and Oil Stocks in the DJIA, 1970 versus 1964

		1963			*1970*	
	Closing Price	Earned Per Share	P/E Ratio	Closing Price	Earned Per Share	P/E Ratio
Chemical companies:						
Allied Chemical	55	2.77	19.8 ×	24⅛	1.56	15.5 ×
Du Pont[a]	77	6.55	23.5	133½	6.76	19.8
Union Carbide[b]	60¼	2.66	22.7	40	2.60	15.4
			25.3 ave.			
Oil companies:						
Standard Oil of Cal.	59½	4.50	13.2 ×	54½	5.36	10.2 ×
Standard Oil of N.J.	76	4.74	16.0	73½	5.90	12.4
Texaco[b]	35	2.15	16.3	35	3.02	11.6
			15.3 ave.			

[a] 1963 figures adjusted for distribution of General Motors shares.

[b] 1963 figures adjusted for subsequent stock splits.

2. *Management.* On Wall Street a great deal is constantly said on this subject, but little that is really helpful. Until objective, quantitative, and reasonably reliable tests of managerial competence are devised and applied, this factor will continue to be looked at through a fog. It is fair to assume that an outstandingly successful company has unusually good management. This will have shown itself already in the past record; it will show up again in the estimates for the next five years, and once more in the previously discussed factor of long-term prospects. The tendency to count it still another time as a separate bullish consideration can easily lead to expensive overvaluations. The management factor is most useful, we think, in those cases in which a recent change has taken place that has not yet had the time to show its significance in the actual figures.

Two spectacular occurrences of this kind were associated with the Chrysler Motor Corporation. The first took place as far back as 1921, when Walter Chrysler took command of the almost moribund Maxwell Motors, and in a few years made it a large and highly profitable enterprise, while numerous other automobile companies were forced out of business. The second happened as recently as 1962, when Chrysler had fallen far from its once high estate and the stock was selling at its lowest price in many years. Then new interests, associated with Consolidation Coal, took over the reins. The earnings advanced from the 1961 figure of $1.24 per share to the equivalent of $17 in 1963, and the price rose from a low of 38½ in 1962 to the equivalent of nearly 200 the very next year.[6]

3. *Financial Strength and Capital Structure.* Stock of a company with a lot of surplus cash and nothing ahead of the common is clearly a better purchase (at the same price) than another one with the same per share earnings but large bank loans and senior securities. Such factors are properly and carefully taken into account by security analysts. A modest amount of bonds or preferred stock,

---

performance of 1) the market as a whole, 2) industry sectors, and 3) specific stocks. As Graham points out, the odds that individual investors can do any better are not good. The intelligent investor excels by making decisions that are not dependent on the accuracy of anybody's forecasts, including his or her own. (See Chapter 8.)

however, is not necessarily a disadvantage to the common, nor is the moderate use of seasonal bank credit. (Incidentally, a top-heavy structure—too little common stock in relation to bonds and preferred—may under favorable conditions make for a huge *speculative* profit in the common. This is the factor known as "leverage.")

4. *Dividend Record.* One of the most persuasive tests of high quality is an uninterrupted record of dividend payments going back over many years. We think that a record of continuous dividend payments for the last 20 years or more is an important plus factor in the company's quality rating. Indeed the defensive investor might be justified in limiting his purchases to those meeting this test.

5. *Current Dividend Rate.* This, our last additional factor, is the most difficult one to deal with in satisfactory fashion. Fortunately, the majority of companies have come to follow what may be called a standard dividend policy. This has meant the distribution of about two-thirds of their average earnings, except that in the recent period of high profits and inflationary demands for more capital the figure has tended to be lower. (In 1969 it was 59.5% for the stocks in the Dow Jones average, and 55% for all American corporations.)* Where the dividend bears a normal relationship to the earnings, the valuation may be made on either basis without substantially affecting the result. For example, a typical secondary company with expected average earnings of $3 and an expected dividend of $2 may be valued at either 12 times its earnings or 18 times its dividend, to yield a value of 36 in both cases.

However, an increasing number of growth companies are departing from the once standard policy of paying out 60% or more of earnings in dividends, on the grounds that the sharehold-

---

* This figure, now known as the "dividend payout ratio," has dropped considerably since Graham's day as American tax law discouraged investors from seeking, and corporations from paying, dividends. As of year-end 2002, the payout ratio stood at 34.1% for the S & P 500-stock index and, as recently as April 2000, it hit an all-time low of just 25.3%. (See www.barra.com/research/fundamentals.asp.) We discuss dividend policy more thoroughly in the commentary on Chapter 19.

ers' interests will be better served by retaining nearly all the profits to finance expansion. The issue presents problems and requires careful distinctions. We have decided to defer our discussion of the vital question of proper dividend policy to a later section—Chapter 19—where we shall deal with it as a part of the general problem of management-shareholder relations.

Capitalization Rates for Growth Stocks

Most of the writing of security analysts on formal appraisals relates to the valuation of growth stocks. Our study of the various methods has led us to suggest a foreshortened and quite simple formula for the valuation of growth stocks, which is intended to produce figures fairly close to those resulting from the more refined mathematical calculations. Our formula is:

$$\text{Value} = \text{Current (Normal) Earnings} \times (8.5 \text{ plus twice the expected annual growth rate})$$

The growth figure should be that expected over the next seven to ten years.[7]

In Table 11-4 we show how our formula works out for various rates of assumed growth. It is easy to make the converse calculation and to determine what rate of growth is anticipated by the current market price, assuming our formula is valid. In our last edition we made that calculation for the DJIA and for six important stock issues. These figures are reproduced in Table 11-5. We commented at the time:

> The difference between the implicit 32.4% annual growth rate for Xerox and the extremely modest 2.8% for General Motors is indeed striking. It is explainable in part by the stock market's feeling that General Motors' 1963 earnings—the largest for any corporation in history—can be maintained with difficulty and exceeded only modestly at best. The price earnings ratio of Xerox, on the other hand, is quite representative of speculative enthusiasm fastened upon a company of great achievement and perhaps still greater promise.
>
> The implicit or expected growth rate of 5.1% for the DJIA com-

TABLE 11-4 Annual Earnings Multipliers Based on Expected Growth Rates, Based on a Simplified Formula

Expected growth rate	0.0%	2.5%	5.0%	7.2%	10.0%	14.3%	20.0%
Growth in 10 years	0.0	28.0%	63.0%	100.0%	159.0%	280.0%	319.0%
Multiplier of current earnings	8.5	13.5	18.5	22.9	28.5	37.1	48.5

TABLE 11-5 Implicit or Expected Growth Rates, December 1963 and December 1969

Issue	P/E Ratio, 1963	Projected[a] Growth Rate, 1963	Earned Per Share 1963	Earned Per Share 1969	Actual Annual Growth, 1963–1969	P/E Ratio, 1969	Projected[a] Growth Rate, 1969
American Tel. & Tel.	23.0 ×	7.3%	3.03	4.00	4.75%	12.2 ×	1.8%
General Electric	29.0	10.3	3.00	3.79[b]	4.0	20.4	6.0
General Motors	14.1	2.8	5.55	5.95	1.17	11.6	1.6
IBM	38.5	15.0	3.48[c]	8.21	16.0	44.4	17.9
International Harvester	13.2	2.4	2.29[c]	2.30	0.1	10.8	1.1
Xerox	25.0	32.4	.38[c]	2.08	29.2	50.8	21.2
DJIA	18.6	5.1	41.11	57.02	5.5	14.0	2.8

[a] Based on formula on p. 295.
[b] Average of 1968 and 1970, since 1969 earnings were reduced by strike.
[c] Adjusted for stock splits.

pares with an actual annual increase of 3.4% (compounded) between 1951–1953 and 1961–1963.

We should have added a caution somewhat as follows: The valuations of expected high-growth stocks are necessarily on the low side, if we were to assume these growth rates will actually be realized. In fact, according to the arithmetic, if a company could be assumed to grow at a rate of 8% or more *indefinitely* in the future its value would be infinite, and no price would be too high to pay for the shares. What the valuer actually does in these cases is to introduce a *margin of safety* into his calculations—somewhat as an engineer does in his specifications for a structure. On this basis the purchases would realize his assigned objective (in 1963, a future overall return of 7½% per annum) even if the growth rate actually realized proved substantially less than that projected in the formula. Of course, then, if that rate were actually realized the investor would be sure to enjoy a handsome additional return. There is really no way of valuing a high-growth company (with an expected rate above, say, 8% annually), in which the analyst can make realistic assumptions of *both* the proper multiplier for the current earnings and the expectable multiplier for the future earnings.
As it happened the actual growth for Xerox and IBM proved very close to the high rates implied from our formula. As just explained, this fine showing inevitably produced a large advance in the price of both issues. The growth of the DJIA itself was also about as projected by the 1963 closing market price. But the moderate rate of 5% did not involve the mathematical dilemma of Xerox and IBM. It turned out that the 23% price rise to the end of 1970, plus the 28% in aggregate dividend return received, gave not far from the 7½% annual overall gain posited in our formula. In the case of the other four companies it may suffice to say that their growth did not equal the expectations implied in the 1963 price and that their quotations failed to rise as much as the DJIA. *Warning:* This material is supplied for illustrative purposes only, and because of the inescapable necessity in security analysis to project the future growth rate for most companies studied. Let the reader not be misled into thinking that such projections have any high degree of reliability or, conversely, that future prices can be

counted on to behave accordingly as the prophecies are realized, surpassed, or disappointed.

We should point out that any "scientific," or at least reasonably dependable, stock evaluation based on anticipated future results must take future interest rates into account. A given schedule of expected earnings, or dividends, would have a smaller present value if we assume a higher than if we assume a lower interest structure.* Such assumptions have always been difficult to make with any degree of confidence, and the recent violent swings in long-term interest rates render forecasts of this sort almost presumptuous. Hence we have retained our old formula above, simply because no new one would appear more plausible.

Industry Analysis

Because the general prospects of the enterprise carry major weight in the establishment of market prices, it is natural for the security analyst to devote a great deal of attention to the economic position of the industry and of the individual company in its industry. Studies of this kind can go into unlimited detail. They are sometimes productive of valuable insights into important factors that will be operative in the future and are insufficiently appreciated by the current market. Where a conclusion of that kind can be drawn with a fair degree of confidence, it affords a sound basis for investment decisions.

Our own observation, however, leads us to minimize somewhat the practical value of most of the industry studies that are made available to investors. The material developed is ordinarily of a kind with which the public is already fairly familiar and that has already exerted considerable influence on market quotations.

---

* Why is this? By "the rule of 72," at 10% interest a given amount of money doubles in just over seven years, while at 7% it doubles in just over 10 years. When interest rates are high, the amount of money you need to set aside today to reach a given value in the future is *lower*—since those high interest rates will enable it to grow at a more rapid rate. Thus a rise in interest rates today makes a future stream of earnings or dividends less valuable—since the alternative of investing in bonds has become relatively more attractive.

Rarely does one find a brokerage-house study that points out, with a convincing array of facts, that a popular industry is heading for a fall or that an unpopular one is due to prosper. Wall Street's view of the longer future is notoriously fallible, and this necessarily applies to that important part of its investigations which is directed toward the forecasting of the course of profits in various industries.

We must recognize, however, that the rapid and pervasive growth of technology in recent years is not without major effect on the attitude and the labors of the security analyst. More so than in the past, the progress or retrogression of the typical company in the coming decade may depend on its relation to new products and new processes, which the analyst may have a chance to study and evaluate *in advance*. Thus there is doubtless a promising area for effective work by the analyst, based on field trips, interviews with research men, and on intensive technological investigation on his own. There are hazards connected with investment conclusions derived chiefly from such glimpses into the future, and not supported by presently demonstrable value. Yet there are perhaps equal hazards in sticking closely to the limits of value set by sober calculations resting on actual results. The investor cannot have it both ways. He can be imaginative and play for the big profits that are the reward for vision proved sound by the event; but then he must run a substantial risk of major or minor miscalculation. Or he can be conservative, and refuse to pay more than a minor premium for possibilities as yet unproved; but in that case he must be prepared for the later contemplation of golden opportunities foregone.

A Two-Part Appraisal Process

Let us return for a moment to the idea of valuation or appraisal of a common stock, which we began to discuss above on p. 288. A great deal of reflection on the subject has led us to conclude that this better be done quite differently than is now the established practice. We suggest that analysts work out first what we call the "past-performance value," which is based solely on the past record. This would indicate what the stock would be worth—absolutely, or as a percentage of the DJIA or of the S & P composite—if it is assumed that its relative past performance will continue unchanged in the future. (This includes the assumption that its relative growth rate, as shown in the last seven years, will also continue unchanged over the next seven years.) This process could be carried out mechanically by applying a formula that gives individual weights to past figures for profitability, stability, and growth, and also for current financial condition. The second part of the analysis should consider to what extent the value based solely on past performance should be modified because of new conditions expected in the future.

Such a procedure would divide the work between senior and junior analysts as follows: (1) The senior analyst would set up the formula to apply to all companies generally for determining past-performance value. (2) The junior analysts would work up such factors for the designated companies—pretty much in mechanical fashion. (3) The senior analyst would then determine to what extent a company's performance—absolute or relative—is likely to differ from its past record, and what change should be made in the value to reflect such anticipated changes. It would be best if the senior analyst's report showed both the original valuation and the modified one, with his reasons for the change.

Is a job of this kind worth doing? Our answer is in the affirmative, but our reasons may appear somewhat cynical to the reader. We doubt whether the valuations so reached will prove sufficiently dependable in the case of the typical industrial company, great or small. We shall illustrate the difficulties of this job in our discussion of Aluminum Company of America (ALCOA) in the next chapter. Nonetheless it should be done for such common stocks. Why? First, many security analysts are bound to make current or projected valuations, as part of their daily work. The method we propose should be an improvement on those generally followed today. Secondly, because it should give useful experience and insight to the analysts who practice this method. Thirdly, because work of this kind could produce an invaluable body of recorded experience—as has long been the case in medicine—that may lead to better methods of procedure and a useful knowledge of its possibilities and limitations. The public-utility stocks might well prove an important area in which this approach will show real pragmatic value. Eventually the intelligent analyst will confine himself to those groups in which the future appears reasonably predictable,* or where the margin of safety of past-performance value over current price is so large that he can take his chances on future variations—as he does in selecting well-secured senior securities.

In subsequent chapters we shall supply concrete examples of the application of analytical techniques. But they will only be illustrations. If the reader finds the subject interesting he should pursue it systematically and thoroughly before he considers himself qualified to pass a final buy-or-sell judgment of his own on a security issue.

---

* These industry groups, ideally, would not be overly dependent on such unforeseeable factors as fluctuating interest rates or the future direction of prices for raw materials like oil or metals. Possibilities might be industries like gaming, cosmetics, alcoholic beverages, nursing homes, or waste management.